Dedicated to my children, Anna and Lucas,
and to their hopes for America

Getting America **UnStuck**
The Politics of **Character** & **Craftsmanship**

———

1. Income Inequality - *United States*
2. Civics and Citizenship - *United States*
3. Environmentalism - *United States*

ISBN: 978-1-5323-2487-1 - *softcover*

Contact

CIVIC ★ ＝THOS
B O O K S

steve@americaunstuck.com
americaunstuck.com

Cover Illustration | Jan Black
Book Development Editor | Jan Black

Book Design | timmyroland.com

Getting America UnStuck

The Politics of **Character** & **Craftsmanship**

STEVEN HOWARD **JOHNSON**

CIVIC ★ ETHOS
BOOKS

Table of Contents

Getting
America
UnStuck

The Politics of **Character** & **Craftsmanship**

Getting America Unstuck

"A journey of possibility."

IF AMERICA WERE TRULY A HEALTHY COUNTRY, what would be different? That's not an easy question. These are disorienting times, and we have become a disoriented people. Our current frame of reference isn't adequate to the challenge.

As it happens, as I was in the midst of finishing this manuscript, I became ill with a very disorienting disease. It began as fatigue, mild at first, but then it steadily deepened. After a couple weeks I collapsed completely and was hospitalized. I am told I was semi-conscious during my first four days, but my brain had taken a break from forming memories and I recall none of it.

On the fifth day of my hospital stay, I came around. Looking back, that was the point at which my immune system had finally gained the upper hand. On the seventh day, our doctors provided a diagnosis. I had been infected with the West Nile virus. Apparently, it takes two or three weeks for one's immune system to muster an effective counter-attack.

Even though I am well on my way toward a full recovery, it continues to amaze me how disorienting the journey had been. To go through a four-day crisis and remember nothing? That's never happened to me before. And it leaves me with this thought: West Nile is hardly the only disorienting force that's loose in our world. So much of our larger environment is the work of forces we don't fully understand.

So, if you like, you may think of *Getting America Unstuck* as a book addressed to the larger disorientation of our times. West Nile is a disorienting disease, for those who have it, but it's hardly the only way to become disoriented.

Modern society imposes so many disorientations, it's hard to keep track. Even the best among us are more disoriented than we realize. Our pundits? Our experts? Our political parties? Our news organizations? Our central bankers? Our candidates for office? We find ourselves on an uncertain journey amidst blizzards of conflicting advice. Is there a way to overcome our uncertainties? To bring our journey into better focus?

I think there is.

It's not the disorientation of a mosquito-borne fever that we want to overcome; it's the disorientation of a civic culture that has gotten badly out of date.

So, think. If there's a civic counterpart to a working immune system, what would it be like? It would have to help us find fresh ways of seeing the world, wouldn't it?

So let's acknowledge our civic distress. Things are out of focus and there's no one whom we fully trust. Without better guidance than today's leaders can offer, it won't be easy to recover. Old methods stopped working quite some time ago. It's time for a fresh approach.

In these pages, I will invite you to reframe the challenge of American Stuckness; I will invite you to approach it from a fresh perspective.

But who am I? How do I see Americans as a people; how do I see America as a country?

In my mind's eye, America is a country in which everyone counts. I haven't written this book for a particular slice of people; I have written it with the thought that any American might pick it up and find something in it that makes sense.

All of us are members of this extraordinary nation, citizens of this extraordinary country. Each of us has something to contribute, none of us – by ourselves – have all the answers. And all of us have tendencies to err. We are stronger when all views are listened to and respected. We can't all of us be right, not all the time, but all of us have something to contribute; all of us have the right to feel respected.

As the Pledge of Allegiance reminds us, we are "one nation, under God, indivisible, with liberty and justice for all."

Many years ago, I was a taxi driver for Denver Yellow Cab, and, in time, an officer of our union, the Independent Drivers Association, a union of some eight hundred highly opinionated individualists. As cab drivers, we weren't exactly a microcosm of the whole nation, but we weren't that far off, either. As an officer of our union, and for two years its president, it was my job to listen to everyone. The phrase "liberty and justice for all" always plucks my heartstrings. It calls to mind our group's highly flavored blend of unity and diversity.

To be sure, rising to that standard will always be harder for a nation than it was for several hundred drivers at Denver Yellow Cab – harder, but just as important.

And that insight gives us an important hint about what has gone missing in America today. We have lost touch with the higher meanings of our national adventure. America isn't a prize to be won by the strong and taken away from the weak. America is a blessing that thrives best when all of us contribute to our nation's larger success.

"OK, Steve, fine, but say just a bit more about who you are."

Fair enough. I have had an improvised career that offered me opportunities to learn about America from the top-down perspectives of the well-credentialed, and other opportunities to view America from the bottom-up perspectives of cab drivers and union officers, and also from the middle class perspectives of my Presbyterian Church and my local Rotary Club. I was raised on the advocacy side of American culture in the 1950s and 1960s but have also given volunteer time to the service side of American culture. My dad loved politics and earned a two-year term in Congress from Colorado as I was finishing high school. My wife has a deep respect for public service and for two years ran the General Services Administration for President Obama.

I see government as an art form. It's an essential function in every society and every era; it is up to us to give it wise direction. As an undergraduate at Harvard, I majored in American History. At Stanford, many years later, I earned an MBA. I worked for Cummins Engine. I worked for Bain's consulting arm. I have wrestled with more spreadsheets and models than I care to remember. I have seen organizations succeed because they were wise enough to set transformational goals for themselves; I have seen them falter because they had no interest in journeys of genuine reform.

If advocacy is an art form, if politics is an art form, if government is an art form, then I suppose my life has turned me into something of an art critic.

If there is one bias that really shapes this book, it's my conviction that America's "experts" almost never get to the bottom of anything. Our experts may be clever about the particulars of our current order, but they are constitutionally incurious about America's larger potential. They are good at sticking up for the business models of the day, no matter how flawed; they are much weaker at awakening us to the promise of more wisely designed business models.

Their imaginations don't have enough reach, and, not surprisingly, as we follow their cues, our imaginations often fall short too.

We are a disoriented people because our leaders and our experts collectively inhabit a stunted worldview. The call to dream of a better tomorrow eludes them. Even our most dedicated activists come to the party with flawed worldviews.

If we are to escape the weight of a flawed past, we shall have to give ourselves permission to dream about a genuinely healthier future.

Cruise control politics won't do it. It delivers more and more of the same. Cruise control conservatism? Cruise control liberalism? Two different ways of falling short. Is there a theme? "Bad systems cause good people to do bad things." When we ally ourselves with the prevailing mediocrities, our ambitions shrink and we find ourselves blending in just when we should be pushing back. It's time to stake out a better vision.

Anyway, that's me in a nutshell. One part cab driver. One part geek. One part reformer. And I invite you to join me in the sight-raising adventure I explore here. America doesn't have to be stuck; America doesn't have to be disoriented. What's the cure and how shall we become part of it?"

Now back to the main thread – America's stuckness and how to overcome it.

Our stuckness is symptomatic of deficiencies in our civic ethos that we haven't wanted to confront.

One of those complexities is the presence of systemic corruption. We don't know how to call it out; we don't know how to blow the whistle.

Another complexity is the need for systemic diagnoses and the need for systemic repair. Systemic perspectives don't come naturally; they are part of a higher art form that few of us have been trained to practice.

Getting unstuck begins inside our hearts. It begins when we finally say "No" to our most corrupted temptations. It expands as we say "Yes" to our larger responsibilities. History has put us on the hook and we should be grateful that it has. As Americans, we are on a hero's journey. We begin as reluctant heroes. We know that we have a calling, but our calling makes us nervous and we wish we could escape its reach.

And then, in time, the larger promise of our calling finally sinks in. Our reformer's calling may feel like a burden, but it is also our dearest gift. As a people, aren't we striving to come of age? And to come of age, won't we first have to acknowledge History's calling? Haven't we been called by History to free America from its stuckness?

Yes, History can be a hard master. Sometimes it gives the hero's journey just to a few – think Churchill and Roosevelt in World War II - and sometimes it gives the hero's journey to entire peoples as well, as the Brits and the Yanks learned so well during World War II.

And what of today? Are we paying any attention to what History needs from us? Or not?

History's journey – with our help – is meant to pull America toward a higher and better path.

But the journey ahead won't be easy. There's so much stuckness to deal with. And we aren't as ready to get our bearings as we could be. That's what this book is for – scoping out the challenges ahead, scoping out our promise.

Chapter One is the Stuckness chapter, the chapter where we bring into focus some of our country's most troubling shortcomings. Our nation isn't just "stuck" – "getting stuck" can be temporary – instead as these examples will suggest, we have pushed our shortcomings to the edge. We have turned "stuckness" into an all-too-permanent reality. A hero's journey may be calling, but we've become too rattled to pay attention.

At the moment, we are so entrenched in our partisan habits that our stuckness has become self-perpetuating. Partisan traditions have been with us for more than two centuries, and from those traditions we have become habituated to the practice of defining ourselves by our interests, our values, and our affiliations. To be a "liberal" or a "progressive" is to have one set of values and interests; to be a "conservative" is to prefer different values and interests. We have been taught to see "politics" as a struggle between interest groups, in which electoral majorities get to strengthen the values they care about and weaken the values they dislike. If liberals are one up, conservatives have to see themselves as being one down. And vice versa. One identity "wins" and the other one "loses."

From force of habit we have come to believe this is our permanent way of life. It doesn't have to be. The larger goal of this book is to describe the civic ethos of tomorrow, the core template from which we fashion America's wiser future. There are alternatives, superior ways of seeing ourselves as citizens. In chapters ahead, I will make the case for a fresh approach.

But to begin, we will start with the numbers, with today's troubling realities. To know our options, we must first know our present situation.

Ready for a starter course in civic self-mastery?

Read on.

Steven Howard Johnson
November, 2016

★

As **Americans**,
we are on a hero's
journey *from* systemic
corruption
to systemic
healing.

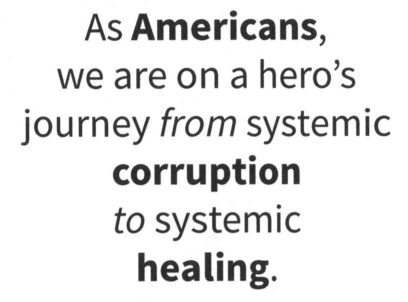

Getting America **UnStuck**
The Politics of **Character** *&* **Craftsmanship**

americaunstuck.com

Chapter One

American Stuckness

ON SO MANY FRONTS

"If they can't explain the numbers, they shouldn't be President."

IF I'M FEELING LOW, I visit the doctor. I get my blood pressure checked, my temperature taken, my pulse counted, my weight measured. The doctor peers into my mouth, listens to my heart, and checks for other warning signs. If there's a larger issue to pursue, he sends me to the lab for a blood test. And now, if I wish to keep track of my daily exercise, I can wear a gadget that will count the number of steps I walk each day. Numbers, numbers, numbers. We assess our health by checking our numbers.

And so it is with America. We can assess America's well being by checking its numbers. This is likely to be an unsettling experience. America's numbers don't tell a story of good health; they tell a story of serious stuckness. Not just stuckness on one or two fronts, but of stuckness on quite a number of fronts. It's time to take a serious second look at how we're doing. We don't know how to bring our current situation into focus; we are not taking care of America as well as we might.

Stuckness: Deficits from 1947 to 2014

Congress has taken a lot of knocks in recent years, so much so that it might have escaped our attention that the United States Congress once lived to an exemplary standard of fiscal responsibility.

1

In the following chart, Fig. 1.1 *Congress' Fiscal Track Record*, I display the contrast between two periods of Congressional fiscal performance, an exemplary period of twenty-six years following the end of World War II, and then a somewhat more irresponsible period that began in the early 1970s and continues even today.

In the twenty-six budget years 1947-1972, Congress ran fiscal surpluses eight times. It ran deficits smaller than one percent of GDP on ten occasions, deficits between one and two percent on four occasions, and deficits of two to three percent on four more occasions. No deficit during that period exceeded three percent of GDP.

In the second period, 1973 – 2014, the story changes. Twenty-three of those budget years stayed within the limits set in the earlier period, but not as well. Nineteen budget years – *nineteen* – had deficits exceeding three percent of GDP! In seven of those years, Congress ran deficits that were three to four percent of GDP; in of those eight years, Congress ran deficits that were four to six percent of GDP, and in four of those years, Congress ran deficits that exceeded six percent of GDP.

What explains the dramatic difference in performance between these two periods? There were several factors. In the first postwar period, both parties had just emerged from a war in which their members had worked together in an all-out battle for victory. Both parties blended a mix of conservatives, moderates, and liberals. This blend turned bipartisanship into an internal necessity for both parties, and eased the task of working together on the bipartisan challenge of developing responsible budgets. House and Senate committees were led by people who prided themselves on being fiscally responsible. And congressional districts had not yet been as callously gerrymandered as they are now.

Fig. 1.1 **CONGRESS' FISCAL TRACK RECORD**

1947 - 1972

1973 - 2014

YEARS WE'VE HAD A BUDGET

SURPLUS

8
YRS

4
YRS

YEARS WE'VE HAD A BUDGET

DEFICIT

18
YRS

**Never over
3% of GDP**

38
YRS

**19 yrs: < 3% of GDP
15 yrs: > 3% of GDP
4 yrs: > 6% of GDP**

What Happened? ⟶

Figure 1.1. White House Budgets. Table 1.2-Summary of Receipts, Outlays, and Surpluses or Deficits as Percentage of GDP.

In the 1970s, though, political realignment reshuffled the parties. Conservatives gravitated to the Republican Party, liberals gravitated to the Democratic Party. And gerrymandering reshuffled the nation's congressional districts. Instead of voters choosing the elected officials they wanted, elected officials got to choose the voters they wanted.

The national interest began to fade from view, eclipsed by intense partisanship. Conservatives used borrowed money to finance tax cuts and win approval from their constituents; liberals used borrowed money to finance the social programs their constituents wanted. Deficit-financing was a source of political advantage for both parties.

Fig. 1.1a 𝒲hat 𝒽appened? **1947 - 1972**

PARTIES SERVED
NATIONAL INTERESTS.

• Parties worked together to rebuild after WWII.

• Each party had conservatives, moderates, and liberals.

• Congressional committees took pride in fiscal responsibilty.

• Districts were a natural mix of voters with different opinions.

WE WERE A NATION
GUIDED BY A
MORAL ANCHOR.

Fig. 1.1b 𝒲hat 𝒽appened? **1973 - 2014**

PARTIES SERVED
PARTISAN INTERESTS.

• Parties worked against each other to build agendas.

• Parties re-shuffled: Conservatives went Republican; Liberals went Democratic.

• Conservatives borrowed to grant tax cuts; Liberals borrowed to fund social programs.

• Districts were re-organized into like-minded voter groups.

WE WERE A NATION
GUIDED BY A
PARTISAN ANCHOR.

Structural changes in the party system played a corrupting role. Partisan realignment played a corrupting role. On both sides of the aisle, America's politicians had lost much of their moral anchor.

Note Figure 1.1 again. Once America had Congresses that served the national interest. Those traditions began to disappear in the 1970s. America's fiscal stuckness testifies to our collective loss.

Stuckness: America's Exploding Senior Cohort

You may have heard that America is getting older. But perhaps you haven't seen the hard numbers. Study the next chart, Figure 1.2, drawn from population forecasts prepared by Social Security, and ponder its long-term implications.

It compares the rise in America's seniors, those of us sixty-five-plus in age, with the rise in working age Americans, those of us between twenty and sixty-four. Working age Americans grow in number only slowly; America's senior cohorts grow dramatically.

From 2005 to 2045, Americans in the working age cohort are expected to grow from 180 million to 219 million, a gain of 21%.

Meanwhile, America's population of seniors is expected to grow by an explosive 125%, from 37 million to almost 84 million.

It's a staggering disparity, a tectonic shift, one for which America isn't the least bit ready. Social Security will be hammered; the nation's healthcare budgets will be hammered.

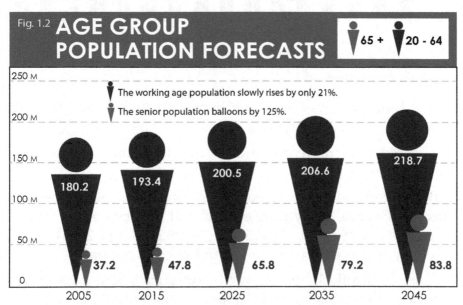

Fig. 1.2 **AGE GROUP POPULATION FORECASTS** 65 +   20 - 64

The working age population slowly rises by only 21%.

The senior population balloons by 125%.

Figure 1.2. Social Security Trustees Report 2015, Table V.A2, Historical, Intermediate Scenario.

Stuckness: Social Security's Predicted Shortfalls

Now to Figure 1.3, and two series of forecasts for America's Social Security program, known formally as OASDI – Old Age, Survivors, and Disability Insurance.

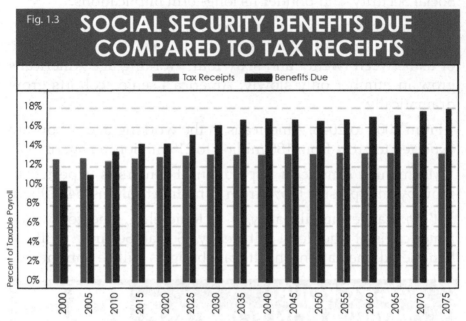

Fig. 1.3 **SOCIAL SECURITY BENEFITS DUE COMPARED TO TAX RECEIPTS**

Figure 1.3. OASDI Trustees Report 2015. Table IV.B1. Historical Data, Intermediate Scenario.

The blue bars represent the expenditure forecast, **Benefits Due**, the program's payouts.

The red bars represent the tax receipts forecast, total **Tax Receipts** expected.

By custom, all such forecasts are stated as percentages of Taxable Payroll, everything earned that falls below the taxable earnings cutoff point ($118,500 in both 2015 and 2016). Social Security updates and reissues both forecasts annually.

This chart reflects the impact of America's Senior Explosion on the nation's Social Security program. Annual Benefits Due have already shot past annual Tax Receipts, and with time they reach nearly eighteen percent of Taxable Payroll.

Meanwhile, given the taxation formulas for Social Security, expected Tax Receipts hold stable at about thirteen percent of Taxable Payroll.

For the moment, Social Security's annual tax shortfalls can be covered from the Social Security Trust Fund. But when the Trust Fund is emptied out, by law Social Security will be obligated to live within its means. In other words, the law will require a steep cut to benefit payments so that the program can be kept solvent.

It's quite a challenge. The working age population that pays taxes to Social Security is expanding only slowly. The retiree population that collects benefits from Social Security is exploding in number. Has America figured out how to deal with this challenge? No. We're in denial. And we're stuck.

Stuckness: Medical Costs As Percent Of GDP

It is often said that the cost of medical care is higher in the United States than it is anywhere else. That's an accurate statement, and there's nothing like a chart to drive the point home. In Figure 1.4, the chart below, I use OECD data on 20 industrialized countries to illustrate yet another aspect of American stuckness. Measured as a percent of GDP, what America spends on medical care is anywhere from forty-eight percent higher to well more than a hundred percent higher than anyone else's medical spending.

South Korea, at 6.9% of GDP for medical care, does the best of the other countries on this chart. The Netherlands, at 11.1% of GDP for medical care, is next to the bottom. At the very bottom is the USA, at 16.9% of GDP.

As you look at this chart, remember that its numbers reflect a time when the size of America's senior cohort is still relatively modest. How might this picture change as the size of the nation's senior population almost doubles?

We don't know. We cross our fingers and pray. Think of this as Stuckness on a truly grand scale.

Fig. 1.4 **MEDICAL SPENDING BY COUNTRY AS PERCENTAGE OF GDP**

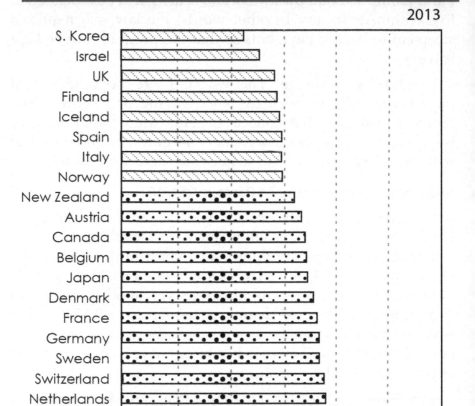

2013

What trends in medical spending might we experience as our senior population almost doubles?

Figure 1.4. OECD Health Statistics 2014. "How Does the United States Compare?"

Stuckness: The Rise of Intentional Inequality

Much has been said about inequality of late. Let's put just a couple of numbers to that conversation. Here I draw on the work of Cal-Berkeley economist Emmanuel Saez, whose Excel spreadsheets on pretax earnings have been derived from IRS digests dating back to the very beginning of the income tax. The following graph, "Shares of Pretax Earnings," has been derived from this source.

Here we examine the pretax earnings of three broad income groups, the Bottom 90%, the Next 9%, and the Top 1%, beginning in 1946 and stretching through 2015. The graph shows us how the relative shares of these three groupings have evolved over time.

From 1946 to the late 1970s one sees a steady distribution of earnings. Those in the Bottom 90% receive sixty-eight percent of the nation's total pretax earnings. Those in the Top 10% receive the remainder.

In the 1980s, the old stability gives way. The squeeze is put on the Bottom 90%, and by 2014, their share of pretax earnings falls from 68% to 52%. Those in the Next 9% and the Top 1% together boost their total share from 32% to 48%.

If we were to characterize both periods, the earlier period and the current period, by the three-way splits they created, we'd describe the earlier economy as a 68-23-9 economy, and we'd describe the current economy as a 52-30-18 economy.

The Bottom Ninety Percent have lost sixteen points, falling from 68% to 52%, its share of the total down by a fifth!

The Top One Percent has picked up ten points. Its share has more than doubled. The Next Nine Percent has picked up five points. Its share has risen by a fifth.

These are not modest shifts on the margins. These numbers tell us a drastic change in the behavior of the American economy. For those in the Top One Percent to more than double their share and for those in the Next Nine Percent to grow their share by a fifth, those in the Bottom Ninety Percent have been forced to accept major cuts in the paychecks they would otherwise have had.

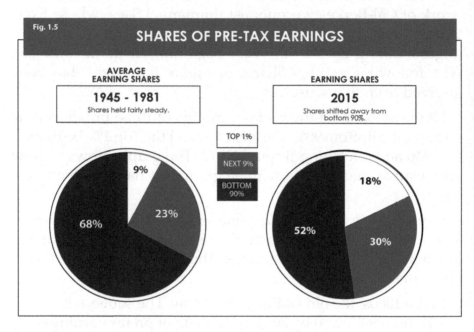

Figure 1.5. Author's calculations drawn from database compiled by Professor Emmanuel Saez. Eml.berkeley.edu/~saez/ Select "Income and Wealth Inequality," then "Tables and Figures Updated to 2015" for the Excel file.

As these new trends have taken hold, there has been a lot of "Let's pretend" from economists. Let's pretend – this was caused by globalization. Let's pretend – this was caused by a growing mismatch between the skills the economy needs and the skills people have. Let's pretend – this was caused by the decline of American manufacturing.

As we will see in greater detail later, there's a better way to explain what happened. *The federal government changed sides.* There was a time when the American economy was guided by an operating system that protected average Americans. Call it the era of FDR's Rules.

Then a new team took over, zeroed out FDR's Rules, and replaced them with Reagan's Rules. The operating system based on FDR's Rules had protected the Bottom 90%. President Reagan's new operating system was focused on enriching the Top 1%.

But it wasn't just Reagan and his Republican team that authored this switch. Democrats played along. They let go of FDR's Rules without putting up the fight that their voters deserved.

It was not by accident that the American Dream has gone dark for working Americans. Those now in charge wanted it to go dark.

More stuckness!

Stuckness: Federal Budget Trends

Let's turn to another set of numbers – to the money America spends through its federal budget for a whole range of functions and purposes. What might we learn?

In the graph below, I have taken a complex table from the Office of Management and Budget and distilled from it six major categories of spending. I suggest we start with the bottom wedge and work upward.

The first wedge reflects the budgets for Defense and for Veterans.

The next wedge reflects spending for the Social Security and Disability programs. The third wedge reflects the Medicare budget and related medical budgets.

The fourth wedge represents support services for the poor, referred to in the federal budget as "Income Security."

The fifth wedge, "All Other Programs," in some ways is the most interesting. If I think about the Federal Government in broad terms, what comes to mind are its cabinet and sub-cabinet functions - State, Treasury, Justice, Transportation, Education, National Science Foundation, the Weather Service, the Patent Office, Housing and Urban Development, Energy, Interior, Labor, Commerce, and so on. The fifth wedge wraps these together and labels them "All Other Programs."

The sixth (and top) wedge represents interest paid on the national debt.

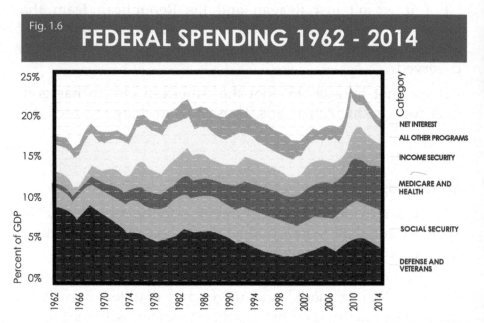

Figure 1.6. Author's analysis, using OMB Tables 8.5, 8.7, and GDP Series hist10z.11

When I look at how these various priorities have changed over time, three major themes catch my eye.

First of all, Defense spending has shrunk, in relative terms. It isn't nearly as sizeable today as it was in the early years of the Cold War. Defense Spending used to absorb ten percent of GDP; today it represents a shade less than five percent.

Second, what one might call "Social Spending" has exploded. When I first put this chart together, I was startled, frankly, by the magnitude of this growth. In 1962, Social Security, Medicare, and Income Security represented about four percent of GDP. Today, half a century later, their relative size has more than tripled, to thirteen percent of GDP. These three budget categories now dominate federal spending.

Third, what's called "All Other Programs" has been squeezed. We have gone through periods when our federal budget committed five percent of GDP to such priorities as Transportation and Education and so on. Today the budget barely musters two percent of GDP to cover this same collection of activities. What one might think of as "The Federal Government" accounts today for barely a tenth of the federal budget. When people say, "The Federal Government is too big," they don't realize that "The Federal Government" in any traditional sense represents barely a tenth of the federal budget.

Let's reflect for a moment on how America's Stuckness is likely to impact these spending patterns.

If we don't get medical stuckness under control, a doubling in the number of elders will intensify the demand for Medicare spending.

An answer for Social Security is essential as well. Current demographic trends in combination with current benefit formulas call for its size to expand by about a third over the next couple generations.

What about poverty rates and "Income Security" spending? If the American economy continues to favor the Top Ten Percent, those in the bottom ninety percent are sure to need increasing amounts of "Income Security" spending. With the advent of Reagan's Rules, the nation's Income Security programs have been put under greater pressure. It's an odd bargain Congress has made. Let the nation's employers off the hook – if they're not paying adequate wages, well, that's their right, isn't it? But that's okay, Congress will make up the difference by using taxpayer dollars to look after the poor. Not a bargain I care for, but it's the bargain that the Congress has backed itself into.

Speaker Paul Ryan promises his supporters a government that "cuts spending" and "cuts taxes." How will he fulfill these two promises as the nation's retiree population doubles in size? How will he fulfill such a promise as the Bottom 90% loses still more ground? Will he take medical coverage away from the elderly? Will he shrink Social Security benefits? Will he cancel support programs for the poor and let them feel even more abandoned by America than they already feel? Will he cut Defense Spending? Will he strip away federal spending for highways?

Or will he break his promises? Will he keep spending high enough to take care of America's needy? Will he raise taxes?

Or will he take on the Top One Percent and fight to restore fairness to the American economy? Creating a fairer economy will make managing the federal budget somewhat easier.

Look at the numbers. In the sort of America that Mr. Ryan wants to create, support for America's elderly and America's underpaid working people will take quite a beating.

Here's my proposed motto for all future elections. "If they can't explain the numbers, we shouldn't vote for them."

Stuckness: Federal Tax Receipts

Now to Federal Tax Receipts over an even longer time period.

The previous dataset begins with 1962. This dataset reaches much further back; I pick up the story in 1945.

Its first wedge, at the bottom of the chart, Corporation Income Taxes start at 7% of GDP but average 4.2% of GDP from 1945 through 1970. From 1980 through 2015, Corporation Income Taxes have averaged only 1.7% of GDP. Corporations don't shoulder nearly as much of the federal government tax load as they used to.

Now shift your attention to the top slice, Excise Taxes & Other. At one time, Excise taxes (whiskey, tariffs, etc.) represented a more significant share of federal revenue, roughly 3.3% of GDP in 1945. But they slowly decline in significance, and by 2015 are only 1.7% of GDP.

With Corporation Income Taxes Shrinking, and Excise Tax Receipts shrinking, the burden grows for Individual Income Taxes, and for Social Insurance and Retirement Receipts, the second and third wedges up from the bottom.

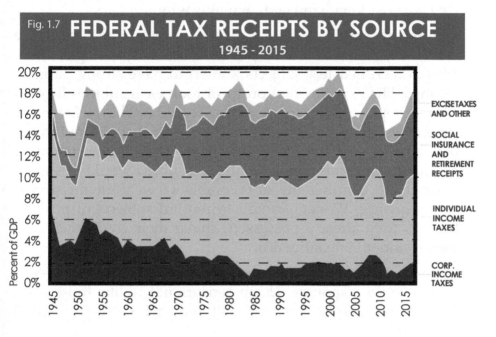

Figure 1.7. Office of Management and Budget, Table 2.3

Individual Income Tax Receipts average 7.7% of GDP across this whole period, with a slight upward trend. From 1945 through 1965, receipts average 7.3% of GDP; from 1995 through 2015, receipts average 7.9% of GDP.

These results leave the third wedge up from the bottom as the one forced to expand the most. And that's what we see. Social Insurance and Retirement Receipts average only 2.1% of GDP from 1945 through 1964. Then from 1965 through 1984, this wedge averages 4.8% of GDP. From 1985 through 2015, it averages 6.2% of GDP. That which was lost in Corporation Income Taxes and in Excise Taxes has been captured through Social Insurance and Retirement Receipts.

Psychological Stuckness

Our stuckness is compounded by our partisanship and the psychological narrowing it creates. Indeed, it's possible that partisanship, as it intensifies, becomes physically addictive. Psychologist Jonathan Haidt explains why.

In his recent book, *The Righteous Mind*, Haidt calls the reader's attention to a telling experiment. Psychologist Drew Westen recruited test subjects known to have strong partisan feelings. His experimental protocol took each subject through a three-step exercise. First, a subject would be shown favorable statements about a public figure that he or she admired. Next, the same subject would be shown an unfavorable statement about the same individual. Finally, the subject would be shown a statement refuting the unfavorable view. With this three-step sequence, Westen wanted to remind subjects of positive feelings they already possessed, shake their confidence, and then restore their confidence.

In each step of this experiment, Westen measured his subject's deeper brain responses. Using sensors not unlike those used in lie detector tests, Westen monitored each subject's visceral responses.

Westen was particularly interested in capturing reactions in a part of the brain known as the ventral striatum, a brain region that's important to our moods.

Jonathan Haidt elaborates:

> *All animal brains are designed to create flashes of pleasure when the animal does something important for its survival, and small pulses of the neurotransmitter dopamine in the ventral striatum (and a few other places) are where these good feelings are manufactured. Heroin and cocaine are addictive because they artificially trigger this dopamine response. Rats who can press a button to deliver electrical stimulation to their reward centers will continue pressing until they collapse from starvation.*

How did Westen's subjects react when shown the third slide, the one aimed at restoring their faith in the individuals they admired? The sensing equipment reported a consistent pattern. In the third step, as the subject's faith is restored, the subject's ventral striatum reacts, releasing dopamine and giving the subject a moment of intense satisfaction.

This finding, Haidt suggests,

> . . . *would explain why extreme partisans are so stubborn, close-minded, and committed to beliefs that often seem bizarre or paranoid. Like rats that cannot stop pressing a button, partisans may simply be unable to stop believing weird things. The partisan brain has been reinforced so many times for performing mental contortions that free it from unwanted beliefs. Extreme partisanship may be literally addictive.*[1]

If Haidt is right, the forces of intense partisanship have drawn us into addictive blind alleys and left us there. In this reading of our situation, addictive partisanship renders its victims incapable of engaging in cause-and-effect reasoning. Does America's stuckness reflect our own personal stuckness?

What We've Been Doing Isn't Working

It has been almost fifty years since the U.S. Congress operated from a clear sense of fiscal responsibility. All sorts of problems have deepened, steadily, without those in charge showing much interest in changing course.

We as a nation are in the grip of several major collisions unfolding in slow motion. The aging of the population is inevitable. Social Security has not been put on a sound footing. The cost of medical care is far higher in America than anywhere else in the world. Meanwhile, the income split between the Bottom 90 and the Top 10 has dramatically fattened earnings

---

1 - Jonathan Haidt, *The Righteous Mind: Why Good People Are Divided by Politics and Religion.* Knopf Doubleday Publishing Group. 2012. p 100-103.

for those at the top while holding back earnings for a majority of the nation's work force.

Every wealthy nation faces a similar challenge. Temptation is eternal. Corruption is a choice.

A wise and alert democracy blows the whistle on systemic corruption. A careless democracy lets itself be distracted, and once the public is properly distracted, the forces of systemic corruption have an easy time capturing the keys to the control room.

In an economy of systemic corruption, the strong enrich themselves without limit, while the weak get cast aside.

In a corrupted political system, politicians win office and hold office by doing the bidding of the super rich.

In a weakened civic culture, too many of us go along in order to get along. The forces of coercive conformity are everywhere, their sheepdogs nipping at our heels to keep us from challenging the party line.

But there's a measure of hope. Tens of millions of Americans can't stand the idea that we are to be trapped by systemic corruption from here forward. They already know that today's system wears a mask, pretending to be something different from what it really is.

If we can take away the mask, if we can figure out the art of wise self-government, we can turn the tide.

For the moment, we are trapped in a political argument that was invented by others and that serves hardly any of America's real needs. It digs us into a deeper hole; it doesn't help us create a wiser and better America. It's time to introduce a wholly different public conversation.

A wise public will ask itself, "If America were truly working properly, what would be different?"

Let's find out what that might mean.

Stuckness is pervasive, a *symptom* that tells us we haven't been up to the challenge of bringing out **America's best.**

Getting America **UnStuck**
The Politics of **Character** & **Craftsmanship**

americaunstuck.com

★

Chapter Two

Towards A Politics

OF CHARACTER & CRAFTSMANSHIP

"Because big corporations don't have Moms keeping them in line."

TOO MUCH STUCKNESS. Our political culture has put itself badly out of sync with our country's larger needs. Choices that would help America get unstuck don't strike the kind of emotional chord for which today's politicians get rewarded. Our conservatives have lost their way; our liberals have lost their way; our lobbyists and our activist groups have also lost their way.

Or to make the same point from another angle: We cannot solve America's most vexing problems from within the bad habits of the present. What's missing is a larger framework, a larger set of principles or guidelines that will infuse our decisions with enough societal wisdom to keep us out of trouble.

We have never cared to create such a set of higher principles.

Instead, we improvise, decade after decade, generation after generation, according to the fashions of our time. And that's why we're stuck – too much self-interested improvisation, not enough underlying character or wisdom.

What I will argue here is that there is indeed a best answer to the guiding principles question, and it is this: For America to realize its full potential, its people will have to master the art of accepting this country's larger responsibilities. Develop a civic ethos of Character and Craftsmanship and we can bring out America's best.

Please notice the two sets of themes that I'm putting to work here. The first is the vital matter of America's civic ethos. By what core values are we to make civic decisions? Character, I will argue, and Craftsmanship. These two principles lie at the heart of a responsible civic ethos.

The second is the vital matter of America's guiding narrative. For the last half century, history gave us a guiding narrative that centered on the struggle for greater rights – greater rights for minorities, greater rights for women, for gays, for lesbians, and so on. This narrative has played a major role in any number of battles, but its relevance to the next fifty years won't be as great.

History has squared up a different narrative for the years ahead. It goes roughly like this: "To fulfill its higher potential, America will want to step up to its larger responsibilities." In an era of vast systems and vast consequences, a narrative of larger responsibilities is fated to become our rising narrative in the years ahead.

Knowing that our democracy needs a better civic ethos is a bit like knowing that it's a good idea for everyone to agree on basic highway rules. Always drive on the right. Always stop for red lights. And so on. Everyone gets to use the road; everyone gets to drive themselves from their own Point A to their own Point B.

And along the way, by observing basic courtesies, we keep ourselves sorted out and we don't run into each other.

The task of getting our self-governing nation to work reasonably well benefits from the same sort of approach.

First, let's ask ourselves what our proper starting point needs to be. Are we all in agreement that we owe our primary loyalty to the nation as a whole, and to its public interest? Or would all of us prefer to give our primary loyalties to a variety of special interests, no matter how corrupt their behavior may be?

I will assume throughout this book that we are better off agreeing that our primary loyalty is the larger best interest of the nation as a whole, and that when the nation works well, our own individual aspirations also have a better chance of being fulfilled.

Second, let's ask ourselves if we are better off seeing life in America as a series of win-win opportunities, where the goal is to create improvements that benefit everyone? Or should we be in the habit of seeing life as a series of win-lose contests, where the goal is narrow victory for one's own interest group, no matter how much of a burden others may have to bear as a result?

I will assume that the search for win-win solutions is generally the wiser choice. It's not always the easier choice, but more often than not it will be the wiser choice.

Third, I will also assume that ours is a society of cause-and-effect systems. The more wisdom we use in putting them together, the more successes America will enjoy over the long run.

Fourth, I will assume that one of history's ancient lessons still holds true. Where there is prosperity, we will always find ourselves in the presence of temptation. We might turn this into a folk saying.

"Prosperity is eternal; Temptation is a choice."

Societies that yield to temptation find themselves sinking into corruption.

Societies that keep temptation in check also keep corruption in check. They enjoy greater well-being than societies that take the darker path. The Old Testament warns us against corruption, again and again. Nations that heed its warnings are healthier; nations that embrace systemic corruption end up far more damaged.

Four sets of choices for any self-governing people. Our better options can help us unwind our harder problems. Our darker options tempt us to deepen our troubles.

- Should the Public Interest come first? Or the claims of special interests?

- Do we take a Win-Win approach toward Public Life? Or a Win-Lose approach?

- Do we base our choices on Cause-and-Effect Reasoning? Or not?

- Do we aspire to become a society of good Character? Or do we accept a future of Systemic Corruption?

These are like rules of the road, if you will. When we stop on red and go on green, things work better. When everyone drives on the right (or when everyone drives on the left) we avoid accidents and we get where we want to go. And the same goes for these larger codes of civic life.

Our current stuckness stems from an unsolved contradiction. If we are to get ourselves unstuck, we will have to see ourselves as voters who prefer the public interest, and favor politicians who see themselves as responsible to the public interest. But it's not easy for us to lean toward the public interest, and it's not easy for politicians to get elected by promising to govern in the public interest. Candidates on both sides get themselves elected by promising to protect the special interests favored by powerful voting blocs.

An important factor in America's stuckness, therefore, are the choices by which we shape our civic ethos. Wise choices help America fulfill its greater promise; flawed choices intensify our stuckness.

For now, let's start at the beginning. Let's examine what we might learn from a civic ethos of genuine maturity.

For me, this is a path that began to unfold with a tough lesson my Mom hammered home, many years ago.

Our Moms Are Wiser Than We Realize

When I was a boy of four in southeast Denver, I lived with my parents and sister in a modest apartment house. One afternoon I stepped out the back door and glanced around. There, to my left, was a white sheet hanging from a clothesline. There, to my right, gray ashes tumbled from an incinerator. My eyes lit up. What an opportunity!

I grabbed a handful of ashes and flung them against the white sheet. Wow! Another handful! And another! Nothing like tapping one's inner urge to make a mess. I raced inside to share my exciting find with my mom.

Hoo-eee, did I push her button, or what? She was so mad! She hauled me off to apologize to our neighbor. Then gave me a paddling. She had a message to deliver, and I think my four-year-old self actually took some of it in. I had behaved in a way that hurt someone else. I had made a bad choice. I was responsible for my behavior, and for the consequences it created.

As best I remember, it was the first time I had been slammed up against one of life's basic rules. *Behaviors have Consequences. If I do something harmful, I am to accept Responsibility.*

This is such a core lesson! Sooner or later, most of us mess up, and when we do, our moms or our dads let us have it. With luck, and repeated reinforcement, the lesson they're trying to teach takes hold and helps shape our character. If enough of us soak up the same lesson, it becomes part of the moral order by which families and communities hold themselves together.

In healthy communities, the lesson that we are Responsible for the Consequences of our Behaviors will get passed along from one generation to the next.

We do this for others; they do this for us. It's how local communities hang together and stay healthy.

Does the Same Principle Apply to Our Larger Society?

If a Wall Street bank creates a mortgage-backed security, stuffs it full of smelly mortgages, bullies a ratings agency into calling it Triple-A, and sells its nicely-wrapped time bomb to a willing customer, has it imitated my behavior? Has it stuck its hands in a pile of ashes and flung them against someone else's clean sheets?

I think we have to say "Yes," and then some. The same broad principles are just as relevant to banks as they are to four-year-olds. The ill-chosen Behaviors of the banking system had Consequences – damaging consequences. By any rational standard, the banking industry after the Crash of 2008 should have been given a paddling and forced to compensate everyone it had wronged.

But the point I am really after is somewhat larger. Ours is a cause-and-effect world, one that operates at vast scales. Misbehavior, at vast scale, will have harmful Consequences, also at vast scale. It's not enough to say, "Well, that industry serves an important market." It's important for industry – any industry, all industries – not to cause terrible damage along the way.

And it's also important for our civic culture to imitate my mom in another respect. Yes, I was the one who had done wrong, but she also felt responsible. In her mind, she was ultimately responsible for my behavior, and for any harm that I might have caused.

And so it is for our society, taken as a whole. Society, as a whole, has to be the Mom. Or the Dad. If a major industry misbehaves and causes terrible harm, that's partly on us, all of us. After all, we let it happen. It's up to us – "Society" - to accept Responsibility just as my mom accepted Responsibility, up to us to make sure that the guilty industry won't continue to misbehave.

Now let's return to the matter of society's larger size.

Our world is a cause-and-effect place. Think of Behaviors as "causes." Think of Consequences as "effects." Think of Responsibility as something that applies to both. In other words, each industry is Responsible not only for its Behaviors in the market, but also for the Consequences those Behaviors generate. Each industry is responsible both for the "Causes" it sets in motion and also for the "Effects" that trail in its wake.

Now let's tie this basic idea to the core principle of Character.

Character involves the regular acceptance of Responsibility, on the part of players who operate at major scale.

We, the public, are a significant force. We are a society of Character when we accept public Responsibility for how well our society behaves.

This isn't a one-time thing, a switch we throw and then ignore. It's a daily challenge. It is through the consistent acceptance of Responsibility that one builds Character. This is not a new idea; it was one of Aristotle's central arguments. It has echoed through the ages, and been reinforced recently in the writings of David Brooks.[1]

But Responsibility for what? How are we to visualize the full reach of the public's Responsibility?

Let's try this on as our answer: Three-Sixty Responsibility.

Three-Sixty Responsibility

Three-Sixty Responsibility takes in America as a whole. Quite a challenge. How can anyone visualize America as a whole, let alone take responsibility for its larger well-being?

We will have to simplify.

Let's begin by visualizing "America At Work." Nine-to-five. Seven-to-four. The second shift, the night shift, weekend work,

---

1 - David Brooks. *The Road to Character*. Random House. 2015.

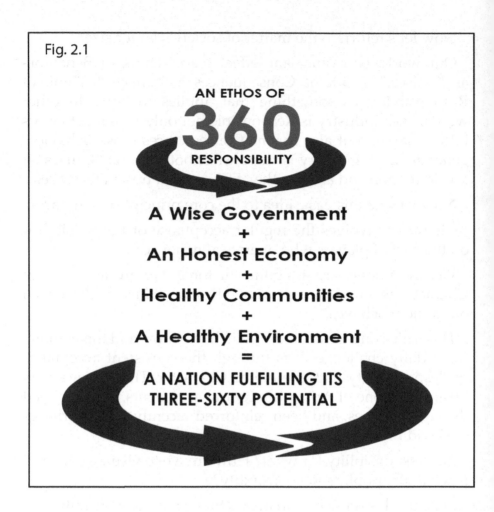

Fig. 2.1

AN ETHOS OF

360

RESPONSIBILITY

A Wise Government
+
An Honest Economy
+
Healthy Communities
+
A Healthy Environment
=
A NATION FULFILLING ITS
THREE-SIXTY POTENTIAL

weekday work. Companies of all kinds, government agencies of all kinds, nonprofits of all kinds.

Let's visualize people coming together at their places of work, gathering resources, producing goods, delivering services, making sales, meeting payrolls, managing investments, and so on.

What emerges in this simple visualization is a rough sense of *Workplace America*, stretching from Hawaii to Maine, from Alaska to Florida. Vast and complex, with big companies and small and so many in between. Think of America at Work as part of our Three-Sixty Responsibility. If America at Work is a thriving place, then part of our Responsibility has been fulfilled.

Hold this thought for another few seconds. Then let it go.

Now visualize "America After Work." America At Play. America in its leisure hours. People at home with their families. Folks socializing and picnicking and going on trips. Fishing, hunting, boating, hiking, grilling, partying.

We are a nation of households, of families, of neighborhoods and communities, and all the places people live. Big cities, small towns, out in the country.

We are a nation of parks and ball fields and swimming pools and tennis courts. We are a nation of streams and rivers and lakes, a nation of plains and hills and mountains. We are a nation of resources – agricultural resources, extractive resources, forestry resources, fishery resources. We are a nation of harbors and seaports, of airports and train stations and subway systems. We are a nation of reservoirs and water treatment plants and water mains, a nation of sewer systems and sewage treatment plants and on and on.

In visualizing "America After Work" we have been visualizing *Asset America*. Community assets. Infrastructure assets. People assets. Environmental and natural resource assets.

America after work. Hold that thought for a few seconds. Now let it go.

For our third exercise, let's visualize America as a self-governing nation-state. As with any state, America has a government of laws, some of them written by Congress or its legislatures and city councils, some of them derived from court decisions. Its elected officials ran for office and won votes by sharing with the public their narratives for how they believe their communities ought to work.

America has a government of agencies, responsible for everything from highways and street lights to national forests to ports and harbors to the collection of taxes and the spending of public funds. America has systems for choosing elected officials to write its laws, for choosing executives to administer its agencies, and for choosing magistrates and judges.

Companies find it easier to do business when they can trust courts to enforce laws of contract. Citizens find it easier to get around when they can trust the state to build highways and maintain stop lights at intersections. Residents find it easier to live in a state that's good at supplying safe drinking water and carrying away sewage. The people as a whole find it easier to live in a nation that's capable of defending itself when attacked.

In visualizing America as a Governed (and self-governing) Republic, we have been envisioning *Civic America.*

How are we to measure these various Americas – Workplace America, Asset America, Civic America?

We measure Workplace America by measuring Gross Domestic Product. Seventeen trillion dollars. Eighteen trillion. Nineteen trillion. The Commerce Department essentially rolls together the Income Statements of all the nation's companies, nonprofits, and government agencies, adjusts these tallies to eliminate double-counting, and cobbles together the nation's official GDP.

In measuring Asset America, though, this approach – an Income Statement approach – isn't really appropriate. We'd prefer to size up our nation's assets in Balance Sheet terms. What are the nation's community and infrastructure assets worth? What are the nation's environmental and natural assets worth? Are they becoming more or less valuable over time? Healthier or weaker? Is the Balance Sheet improving? Or deteriorating?

And how are we to measure Civic America? Are we to use economic measures alone? Community well-being measures alone? Environmental measures alone? Are we to use global corruption comparisons to size up our capacity for self-governing wisdom? There's no simple answer.

These are Thought Exercises, and the point of them is to help us appreciate the full reach of our public responsibility.

On all these counts, we want America to be a healthy country, do we not? We want commercial well-being – a strong GDP. We want Balance Sheet well-being, in the form of community, environmental, and natural resource well-being. We want civic well-being, measured against some larger set of capability standards.

It's quite a portfolio. Sobering, yes, but also exciting. Such tabulations will help each generation know whether or not it has played its part in helping America thrive.

Let's visualize ourselves as a generation that cares, as a generation that steps up to the plate. In other words, let's visualize ourselves as accepting our Three-Sixty Responsibility for America's larger well-being.

What does this imply? If a spirit of Three-Sixty Responsibility is what we want, what sort of civic ethos will make the most sense?

It will be an ethos that values cause-and-effect reasoning, that values Character, that values Craftsmanship. It will extend that core lesson that we first learn when we are young – our Behaviors have Consequences, and therefore we are to accept Responsibility for the Consequences we helped create.

Craftsmanship: How Rising Success Is To Be Achieved

It's one thing to *feel* a sense of responsibility, especially a sense of Three-Sixty Responsibility. It's quite another to *fulfill* such a responsibility.

Craftsmanship speaks to that responsibility. One starts by acknowledging the presence of the many cause-and-effect systems that hold America together. One then accepts responsibility for the character with which they operate – or, perhaps, for their lack of character. One takes on the challenge of Diagnostic Craftsmanship – getting to the bottom of how well they function, or malfunction, and whether they need further attention.

And finally one takes on the challenge of Prescriptive Craftsmanship. "If this system were designed and operating to its full potential, what would have to be different about how it has been put together?" Sometimes this question leads toward repair of a moderately defective system. Sometimes it may lead us toward the transformational redesign of yesterday's business model.

An America of cause-and-effect systems can be well-designed and wisely put together; it can be a source of Three-Sixty satisfaction.

Or an America of cause-and-effect systems can be held captive by the forces of systemic corruption.

It all hangs on us. Are we a people that treats civic life as an exacting art form, one in which high levels of artistry will bring out our best? Or shall we be a people indifferent to the artistry with which the nation's cause-and-effect systems have been put together?

In our best case scenario, we radiate a sense of Craftsmanship. We want America in all its parts to be well-designed, a source of benefit to all.

A civic ethos of Craftsmanship invites us to bring an artist's zest to our civic responsibilities. An America that has been put together exceptionally well is an America that will earn praise for its superior craftsmanship and superior performance.

Why accept second-rate standards when, with a solid commitment to first-rate craftsmanship, we can help America realize its larger promise?

Here's the hero's challenge: Let's develop a civic ethos that teaches us to accept our three-sixty responsibilities, a civic ethos that teaches us to value craftsmanship, a civic ethos that encourages us to help America realize its higher promise.

These words point us in the right general direction. But we will want more detail. How, specifically, are we to rise to this challenge?

We will be a people that pursues Diagnostic Excellence. We will pursue Prescriptive Excellence. We will look at major systems/industries/sectors and we will apply Tests of Character. We will treat the task of bringing out our nation's best as an artistic challenge, and we will measure ourselves by the artistry we express in rising to this challenge.

Diagnostic Excellence. In the ideal scenario, we will dig ourselves out of our toughest challenges with diagnostic efforts that take us all the way to the bottom of things and give us an accurate read.

That's the ideal. Alas, success remains rare, as upcoming chapters will prove. Our pundits and our experts are known for digging only half-way to the bottom of a problem – *almost every problem* – and then filing reports filled with the sort of conventional wisdom that got us into difficulty to start with. They rarely push their diagnoses all the way to the bottom of the matter. No matter what the issue may be.

We need to set a higher bar. Diagnostic success on the nation's toughest challenges is essential. When mediocrity is our core problem, our experts need to say so. When systemic corruption is at the heart of what's wrong, our diagnosticians need to give it to us straight. Unflinching Craftsmanship is essential. If we can't be bothered to get to the bottom of *anything*, our hero's journey goes nowhere.

Testing for Character. In several chapters to come, I will argue that the status quo is badly flawed, often seriously mediocre, and sometimes badly corrupted. A wise diagnosis will acknowledge those flaws and level with the public. What then?

A wise public applies the Character Test to the sector in question. Does its business model lead to faulty behaviors and harmful consequences?

If the answer is "Yes," this industry fails its Character Test, and we have a prescriptive challenge to address. How is the industry's flawed business model to be redesigned? How are its damaging behaviors to be brought to an end?

Prescriptive Excellence. The concept is simple. Figure out how to fix the business model. Then fix it. Overcome yesterday's faulty habits. Turn the business model around; make it part of our nation's larger strategy for success.

It's an easy principle to state, but difficult to achieve. In today's America, special interests regularly conspire against those who seek wise reforms. Sometimes these special interests have corporate roots; sometimes they belong to major advocacy organizations. If they have a party line about how things are supposed to work, they'll defend their party line by attacking the forces of Character and Craftsmanship. They'll do all they can to defeat those who say they should be held to a higher standard.

Prescriptive Craftsmanship is a tough standard, tougher than we might think. Even the most well-meaning reformers can get led astray by cultures of superficial thinking. They want to reform our schools, but their ideas fall short. They want to reduce economic inequality, but they can't get their arms around the core issues. They want to halt global warming, but their message of reform is poorly reasoned. They want a better medical system, but they can't bring their ideas into focus.

Diagnostic weakness and prescriptive half-measures go together far too often. Our stuckness is sometimes rooted in the corruption of the Bad Guys, but there's another possibility as well. Quite often America's stuckness turns out to be rooted as well in the intellectual laziness of the Good Guys.

Good intentions are seldom enough. Even reformers of honorable motives can lose their focus and find themselves caught in the weeds.

The risk of getting caught in the weeds becomes even more pronounced when the journey of true success is one that requires transformational change. Our instincts teach us to be gradualists, even when the course of gradualism is sure to be the course of perpetual failure.

A willingness to consider transformational change is sometimes essential.

Transformational change is a powerful tool. It begins with a vision of how tomorrow's business model is to work – even if that means a fundamental reworking of how we see the world – and then it is brought into being by an extended series of incremental steps that cumulatively fulfill tomorrow's promise.

I tell just such a story in Chapter Four. Back in the 1980s, Cummins Engine was up against competitors who had already taken a transformational approach to manufacturing. If Cummins was to match their performance, it would first have to match their boldness and their meticulous care. I lived a piece of this story and will share it here.

America's very best schools continue to be created by leaders who possess a transformational spirit. In Chapter Five we will learn what distinguishes the best leaders from conventional reformers of various types.

America's "Inequality" problem was created by an act of reverse transformation, if you will. American capitalism operated within a framework of remarkable fairness for thirty-five years after the Second World War. Then the federal government changed sides. What had been a capitalism of prosperity for the entire workforce became instead a capitalism of enrichment for those at the top. If these priorities are to be reversed, yet another round of transformational change will be essential.

So many of America's larger cities have been hollowed out by ghettoization; so many more have been hollowed out by the disappearance of key employers. Incremental reforms aren't likely to give us the change we need; we will have to stretch our habits and welcome transformational thinking if we are to overcome these challenges.

The abusive profiteering of America's medical sector cannot be overcome with piecemeal reform. The larger promise of American medicine will be realized only through the complex adventure of careful transformation.

America's energy sector is led by companies who desperately want their own industrial future to unfold within a framework of gradual change. But this sector's cause-and-effect business model is too dangerous to be left in force for very much longer. The status quo has become so dangerous that transformational action is our only way out.

And at the heart of our democracy we face a transformational challenge of extraordinary importance. In today's America, the politics of systemic corruption has gained the upper hand on any number of fronts. Bringing an end to systemic corruption has become a vital transformational necessity.

Perhaps you will remember what I said just a few pages back? Transformational change has to be thorough, but it's hardly instantaneous. It's not a matter of entering your favorite beauty parlor as a graying brunette and strutting out a couple hours later as a brand-new blonde. Transformational change can require months or even years of persistent effort, one gradual step at a time, with transformation as its final product.

The Politics of Character and Craftsmanship is the appropriate response to an era of large systems, cause-and-effect forces, and far-reaching consequence. History has given us a new narrative – America realizes its full potential best when it rises to meet its larger Responsibilities.

The Politics of Character and Craftsmanship isn't just a fresh approach to issues; it's a fresh civic ethos, one that's matched to an era of large systems in which wise design is the key to America's long-term fulfillment.

Yesterday's narratives have taught us how to rationalize America's stuckness. The civic ethos we have inherited from the past has become an ethos of rationalized misjudgment. It's time for a wiser civic ethos and time for a wiser guiding narrative. In a world of cause-and-effect systems, there's no substitute for Character and Craftsmanship as America's guiding standards. We have to get real. There is a cause-and-effect relationship between the standards we set for ourselves today and the kind of nation America becomes in the years ahead.

Our moms could have told us that. Maybe we ought to have asked them.

Pursue
the larger good,
everyone thrives.

Pursue
narrow self-interest,
everyone suffers.

Chapter Three

Why Have We
GOTTEN SO BADLY OFF TRACK?

"How America's stuckness came to be."

WHY HAVE OUR POLITICS GOTTEN SO OUT OF SYNC with our country's needs?

It wasn't always this way.

In World War II, the nation came together to fight a difficult and bloody war. And from that wrenching journey, Americans emerged with more patriotic solidarity than they had known in a long time.

And that larger mood carried both parties forward for a time. But such a spirit does wear off. Even an experience as profound as World War Two eventually recedes in everyone's memory. America's spirit of national unity was not to last, and there were a host of changes that caused its fraying.

America's Social Revolution

By the 1940s and the 1950s, it had become time for Americans to come to grips with an internal social crisis. White supremacy was no longer an acceptable standard. It was time for Americans of color to have their rights respected, not just in a portion of the nation, but in all its parts.

The journey to reach that point was sure to be wrenching and turbulent. And so it has been. For those steeped in the values of white supremacy since childhood, letting go would prove to be hard, very hard, even though it had become a national imperative.

The spirit of social revolution that began by calling racial segregation into question saw its scope widen, by degrees, into a critique of male supremacy. In the emerging social order of our postwar nation, blatant discrimination against women could no longer be sustained. Change came on many fronts. Women were to become the equals of men in marriage, in the workplace, in college sports, in the military, and, who could tell, perhaps eventually in the White House. The journey of gender equality has come a long way, but has yet to be fully won.

Discrimination against gays and lesbians and transgender individuals was also due to lose its footing. At our church, we made the shift to being open and affirming and, guess what? We're stronger than ever. Our organist/choir director is enormously talented; we are so lucky to have him. He has been in a committed gay relationship for years. For such a long time, as his career unfolded, he'd find himself playing the organ for wedding ceremonies that united straight couples in marriage. "I can play for the weddings of others," he'd say to himself, "but I'll never have a wedding of my own."

Here in Maryland, voters legalized gay marriage in a 2012 referendum. Shortly afterwards, our church adjusted its rules to welcome gay marriage. We were a step ahead of our denomination, whose rules hadn't quite reached that point, but we asked ourselves whether it was worse to be guilty of intolerance or to be guilty of disobedience.

We decided that being guilty of intolerance was worse, and so we changed our rules, an act that foreshadowed a change the denomination would soon be making on its own. In the spring of 2013, our pastor united Bob and Steve in marriage, and finally our organist was able to marry his partner in a wedding that had long been one of his fondest wishes!

Such changes will not go down easily for everyone. Social traditions that have held for generations are not always easy to rework. Pope Francis has loosened things up, just a bit, with his warmth and charm. "Let's try loving everyone," his actions say, "especially those who have been on the sidelines for so long."

America's social revolution still has its dark side. Even as America's middle class neighborhoods have become more multi-racial, many of the nation's poor still live in ghettoized neighborhoods. Poverty zip codes have arisen in all parts of this nation, and all of them suffer from the same ailments. Stable marriages and two parent households are rare. Poor children are at a disadvantage from the start, a disadvantage that widens with time. Inclusion may have become the rule for middle and upper middle class Americans, and we're glad it has, but it hasn't been the rule for poor Americans. Exclusion has become one of the hard realities of our time, and in a way it too is color-blind. Everyone who's poor gets hurt.

These changes have been a source of turbulence; many communities that value traditional norms are still upset. But that doesn't mean that Americans have lost a sense of morality; what it means is that ancient Biblical rules simply don't measure up to the higher and more inclusive standards of today. Ours has become an era of aspirational morality. Instead of measuring today's behaviors against an ancient code, we prefer a spirit of brotherhood. In respecting folks of all backgrounds, the admonition to love our brothers as ourselves has led us to an aspirational morality that seeks to create a climate of respect among people of all colors and languages and backgrounds. Ancient traditions thrived on prejudice and exclusion. Aspirational morality aspires to a community spirit of inclusion and mutual respect. Every time we pledge our allegiance to the principles of "Liberty and Justice For All," we separate ourselves just a little further from the tribal codes of a much earlier time.

Odds are we will emerge from this transition with a new blend of traditional morality and aspirational morality, with a blend that still celebrates the two-parent family as well as single-parent families, that respects women as the equals of men, that respects Americans of all colors and ethnicities, that respects LGBT Americans and heterosexual Americans with equal enthusiasm.

Political Realignment

In the 1860 election, the Republican candidate for President defeated the Democratic candidate. The party of Abraham Lincoln had defeated the party of Thomas Jefferson. At issue was the role of slavery in America's future. Lincoln declared that the United States could not continue to be a nation that was half-slave and half-free. It was time for the nation to bring slavery to an end.

Not long after, eleven southern states voted to secede. Confederate troops in South Carolina attacked Fort Sumter. An inflamed North rallied to the Union cause, triggering a brutal Civil War in which Union forces prevailed. The secessionists surrendered, and a bloodied nation began to lick its wounds and inch its way back toward sanity. Southerners of that era hated the Republican Party and for many decades thereafter placed themselves solidly in the Democratic camp.

And in one of the odd outcomes of that era, both parties came to include within their ranks politicians of nearly all persuasions. There were conservatives in both parties, moderates in both parties, and liberals in both. The Democratic Party's most conservative members were far to the right of the Republican Party's most liberal members. Both parties, in different ways, were big tent parties.

Despite their similarities, the parties clashed heatedly in every decade. The Great Depression came as a shock to the nation, and then the Second World War as an even more profound shock. Americans had to rally across lines of party, class, and region to fight and win the war, and in Congress both parties emerged from the war with a stronger sense of cross-party loyalty and civility than usual.

Partly as a result of the ideological blending that marked both major parties, the U.S. Congress was to practice greater fiscal discipline in the 1940s, 1950s, and 1960s than it has since. Politicians in both parties pleaded their causes with appeals to the national interest. Both parties respected the need for cause-and-effect reasoning, and standards of legislative courtesy were high. Almost all members of the House and Senate moved their families to the Washington area, and friendships "across the aisle" were not uncommon.

Through diligence and a large stroke of luck, my dad got himself elected to Congress in 1958, from Colorado's Second District. My parents packed us in a car and the five of us moved to the Washington area. I was in high school, my sister in junior high, and my brother in grade school. I remember my dad telling stories about the courtesies that were the standard by which House members conducted business. Did someone rise to speak on a point? The conventions of the time required the other member to give up the floor by saying, "I yield to the gentleman for whom I have the utmost high regard."

On rare occasions, the tone might shift, if just by a notch. One Congressman – if memory serves, it was Representative Gross of Iowa – insisted on challenging almost every item in the federal budget, no matter how miniscule it might be, and it didn't bother him that everyone else viewed him as a royal pain. On one occasion he asked for the floor yet again, and this was the response he received: "I yield to the Gentleman for whom I have the least measure of utmost high regard."

By the standards of the time, that was as harsh an insult as one could offer. Members of Congress disagreed, sometimes deeply, but they did so from within a culture of great southern courtesy.

My dad's career as a Democrat serving a normally Republican district lasted for only a term. In 1960, he lost his re-election race by a wide margin, though I believe JFK lost in the district that year by an even wider margin.

It wasn't long before the sixties became The Sixties. The Solid South's traditions of white supremacy and racial segregation were badly out of step with the larger culture of postwar America, but no one expected them to be set aside voluntarily. Those activists who disliked segregation, therefore, had to pick a very serious fight on this issue if they were to have any chance of winning the changes they sought. In a wise move, the nation's civil rights leaders made a point of waging their freedom struggle from within a blended tradition of Christian pacifism and Gandhian non-violent resistance.

And then, for the first time in history, the South would find its traditions of violent suppression displayed on television for the nation to see. Television cameras introduced the entire nation to the moral disgrace of segregation, not just once, but over and over again. Police dogs. Fire hoses. Arrests. Jailings. Children murdered in church bombings. College-age community organizers kidnapped and killed. With each new outrage, segregation's legitimacy shrank, and shrank; freedom's cause grew stronger.

In 1964 President Johnson asked Congress to pass the Civil Rights Act and Congress agreed. In 1965 President Johnson asked Congress to pass the Voting Rights Act. That, too, was approved.

And the raison d'être for the Solid South was no more. The Republicans had always been the party of civil rights; the Democrats had always been the party that protected Jim Crow. With passage of America's new Civil Rights laws, it was only a matter of time before both parties underwent significant realignment.

Northern liberals who had once been Republicans when the Republican Party was the party of civil rights found themselves becoming Democrats.

Southern conservatives who had long belonged to the Democratic Party found themselves becoming Republicans.

In an earlier era, there had been extensive overlap, with conservatives, moderates, and liberals in both parties.

By the 1980s the realignment was well under way. Conservatives would soon belong only to the Republican Party. Liberals would soon belong only to the Democratic Party.

While this aspect of the story is well-known, it was accompanied by another shift in power that doesn't get quite as much play. Advocacy movements were on the rise; political bosses were on the decline. On the Democratic side, activists who had come together around civil rights made common cause with activists who had come together to oppose the War in Vietnam. They took on the Democratic Party's aging machine and stripped away much of its former power.

On the Republican side, ideological conservatives launched a movement of their own. The upheaval on the Right wasn't a mirror image of the upheaval on the Left, but in the end, both parties found themselves answering less to those who had been their traditional leaders and more to the passions of their grassroots activists.

And this is where the absence of a shared civic ethos has become a source of increasing dysfunction. America has lost the membership overlaps and civic norms that once compelled partisans in both camps to put the interest of the nation ahead of their ideological loyalties.

Both parties have been spiritually impoverished by the ascent of ideological activism. Where both parties once shared a number of common sentiments, today that sort of bonding has almost disappeared.

Think on that for a moment. What does that tell us about our culture? It tells us that Americans in different parties had been held together more by personal bonds than by the bonds of an underlying civic ethos. With personal ties as the cushion, Americans hadn't been forced to wonder if the nation might not also need a unifying civic ethos. And now that personal ties between the parties have crumbled, we have begun to realize that our instincts haven't served us well. Conservatism is too fierce to draw much empathy from America's liberals; liberalism is too fierce to draw much empathy from America's conservatives.

What we see instead is the rise of in-group liberalism on the left and in-group conservatism on the right. Responsible cause-and-effect reasoning is condemned; raw loyalty is all that really counts. Neither party obligates itself, or its followers, to listen to all the nation's people. Neither party obligates itself to put the national interest first, ahead of partisan and sectional interests. The Republican Party isn't America's party, not any more. It exists to serve its factions, not the American people as a whole. And the Democratic Party suffers from much the same kind of narrowing.

Gerrymandering has intensified even further the narrowing effects of party realignment. In the 1960s, the Supreme Court handed down decisions that outlawed population inequalities among congressional districts and also among legislative districts. From the census of 1970 forward, all states have been required to redraw district boundaries to meet the Supreme Court's equal population standards.

Had this responsibility been given to neutral bodies, its effects would not have been so mischievous. Unfortunately the weight of custom turned this new responsibility over to those most likely to misuse it – the nation's state legislatures. We are now in an era of gerrymandered democracy in which it is standard practice for our elected officials to choose the voters they want. You thought democracy was about voters choosing the elected officials they want? Ah, in today's gerrymandered nation, that's not nearly as true as it used to be.

As an unsavory result, almost all the nation's congressional districts are either reliably red or reliably blue, a practice that intensifies the power of the nation's most impassioned partisans while choking off the voices of the nation's more thoughtful moderates.

This has changed America in yet another way that might not have caught our attention. Let me share a story . . .

A high school friend of mine, Ed Levine, worked for many years on the staff of the Senate Foreign Relations Committee. As he reached his upper sixties, the Senators he had served honored him with a retirement party, held in the same hearing room that's been shown so often on television. John Kerry hoisted himself onto a folding chair and did the honors, expressing his own appreciation for Ed's years of service and inviting several of Ed's colleagues to share their thoughts as well.

It was this event, if memory serves, at which I picked up an interesting piece of Capitol Hill scuttlebutt. It has long been the custom of Senators and Members of Congress to record themselves on video, so that local news organizations will have fresh footage from the state's Senators and Members of Congress. Those who pay attention to such things have noted a distressing change. In the past, it had been the custom for Senators and Members of Congress to stand in front of the Capitol's camera crew and argue the issue of the day with appeals to the national interest.

A nice custom, now abandoned. In today's Capitol, Republican videos routinely appeal only to a conservatives. Videos featuring Democrats are pitched only to liberals. Neither party states its case by appealing to the national interest. Both parties have been cheapened and by now everyone accepts this change as the new normal.

Three interwoven trends: political realignment, the rising power of activist ideologues, and intensified gerrymandering.

And one major result: Today's politicians aren't nearly as concerned about the national interest as were the politicians of earlier generations.

Perhaps now we have a better sense of why America has gotten itself so stuck.

Modern Conservatives Lose Their Way

There are two paths that will draw most of us into thinking about politics. Sometimes we are drawn in with our hearts; sometimes we are drawn in with our heads.

When political leaders wish to speak to our hearts, they will spin out Morality Play tales of some sort, just as Reagan once loved his Morality Plays about honest citizens being stiffed by arrogant government bureaucrats. The goal is to evoke sympathy for someone who is presumably a noble citizen and disgust for someone who is presumably a blinkered bureaucrat.

Should a politician wish to appeal to our minds, they'll set aside the Morality Play approach and make a more traditional case. Facts count. Cause-and-effect reasoning counts. Thoughtful exploration of options might find its way into the discussion.

Both choices can serve us well when we take the national interest as our starting point; neither choice is likely to serve us well if we don't.

While Democrats and Republicans both suffer from a diminished ability to make national interest arguments, Republicans have added an even deeper failing to their repertoire.

Modern Conservatives have given their hearts to Morality Play emotionalism so intensely that their capacity for cause-and-effect reasoning isn't that strong any more.

Five individuals have played especially significant roles in creating the new Conservatism: Friedrich Hayek, Milton Friedman, Ronald Reagan, Grover Norquist, and Newt Gingrich.

Friedrich Hayek (1899-1992) was born in Austria, later became a British citizen, and spent a portion of his career at the University of Chicago. As an economist, he made his mark on several fronts; one of his most influential arguments grew out of lessons he had drawn from watching socialists compete for power in his native Austria. Socialists, he wrote, are ideologues. Put them in power and they will devote all their energies to advancing their ideology. Their ideological loyalties, Hayek warned, will lead them to create more problems than they'll solve.[1] It wasn't a great stretch for Hayek and his American admirers to take that argument and apply it to the Democratic Party with its welfare state sympathies. It was a simple syllogism. Ideologues govern badly; welfare state liberals are ideologues; therefore welfare state liberals will govern badly.

But take note: In the real world, American liberals are not cut from the same cloth as Austrian socialists. The popularity of Hayek's dictum about ideologues owes its appeal among Americans not to its substantive accuracy but to its Morality Play symbolism. It connects with conservatives primarily on an emotional level.

Milton Friedman (1912-2006) wrote an essay in 1970 challenging the idea that business executives were to be held accountable for all sorts of social goals as well as for their business performance.[2] Friedman argued that a CEO was responsible only to his investors, and if he increased shareholder value, he had done his job.

Friedman himself, I suspect, knew that such a principle would have to have qualifiers. I doubt that Friedman would have defended a "whites-only" hiring policy; almost surely he would have agreed that a minimal set of governmental rules are essential for keeping things from getting badly out of line.

But Friedman's core argument was so blunt that no one cared about the possible qualifiers. Here, too, with Friedman's authority backing them up, conservatives appreciated the emotional charge his argument delivered. Shareholder value, Yes! Social responsibility, No! Weston's dopamine receptors are sure to light up in audiences that love Friedman's message.

---

1 - F.A. Hayek, *The Road to Serfdom*. University of Chicago Press. 1944.
2 - http://www.colorado.edu/studentgroups/libertarians/issues/friedman
   -soc-resp-business.html

Ronald Reagan (1911-2004) in the 1970s was regularly on the radio with his own version of Paul Harvey folk wisdom. Arch-conservative Joseph Coors funded Reagan's daily five-minute radio talks, short vignettes in which the Gipper served up an endless supply of anecdotes bearing on the same theme: Government bureaucrats are *always* arrogant; decent citizens *always* get trampled.

When Reagan became President after the 1980 election, he turned his daily radio pitch into the Morality Play slogan that branded his administration: "Government isn't the *solution* to our problems; government *is* the problem."

In this grand but simple-minded gesture, President Reagan cast aside cause-and-effect reasoning as a guiding principle for Republicans. Conservatives from Reagan's day forward have defined themselves by his Morality Play aversion to government. The notion of weighing issues on their merits has largely gotten crowded out.

In 1985, *Grover Norquist* (1956-) founded Americans for Tax Reform to promote tax reduction as a central principle of conservative government. In service of that goal, Norquist and ATR challenged Republican candidates across the nation to sign an anti-tax pledge, committing themselves in office to vote against any and all tax increases.[3]

This was another bold advance for Morality Play politics, another damaging defeat for cause-and-effect reasoning. Norquist's anti-tax pledge caught on. Republican candidates and office-holders agreed that Norquist's anti-tax Morality Play would guide their decision-making from then on. No honorable Conservative would want to come out in favor of cause-and-effect reasoning, not if such thinking might lead to tax increases.

Newt Gingrich (1943-) wrote and distributed a memo to Republican activists in 1994 titled, "Language: A Key

---

3 - Wikipedia article on Grover Norquist.

Mechanism of Control,"[4] in which he urged Republicans always to characterize their opponents in negative terms, and always characterize themselves in positive terms.

How could anyone have paid greater allegiance to Morality Play politics? In Gingrich's scripted demonology, liberals were always to be outfitted in black hats and conservatives in white hats. Might anyone of that era find himself longing for a strong dose of old-fashioned melodrama? In Newt Gingrich's hands, Morality Play melodrama was to become the emotional template for America's Republicans, especially in their political campaigns.

A party that had risen to prominence in 1858 on the strength of Abe Lincoln's performance in the Lincoln-Douglas debates has now become a party whose self-definition is centered on Gingrich's list of pejorative adjectives and the Morality Play imagery those adjectives evoke.

For quite some time, Democrats in the Annapolis area have held weekly breakfast meetings to hear from quite an assortment of local speakers. And, for a period of time, Annapolis area Republicans did much the same. Quite often I attended both sets of breakfast meetings and appreciated the wide range of speakers those breakfasts brought to town.

In the Republican Party's breakfast meetings, it was clear that the Morality Play message of modern conservatism had taken hold. When asked to define themselves, Maryland Republicans regularly called themselves "the party of free markets, small government, low taxes, and individual responsibility."

It's quite something, isn't it, to have a party that that thinks itself qualified to guide a complex nation anchoring itself in something so simplistic. Whatever happened to evidence-based thinking and cause-and-effect reasoning?

The subtext is unsettling: "We are Conservatives. We are unswervingly loyal to our *methods* but we bear no responsibility

---

4 - http://fair.org/extra-online-articles/language:-a-key-mechanism-of-control/

for their wider *consequences*. Keep taxes low, keep markets free, keep government small, and you'll be respected by your Conservative peers."

Or one might say it this way: Conservatives want to be defined by their methods, not by the results their methods produce. "Small government, regardless of results." "Free markets, regardless of consequences." "Low taxes, regardless of society's needs." "Individual responsibility, regardless of how needy the poor and vulnerable may be."

Modern conservatives have taken from Milton Friedman the idea that companies don't have to be held responsible for the consequences of their business practices. This wasn't quite what Friedman said, of course, but it was what conservatives wanted to hear.

Conservatives have taken from Ronald Reagan the idea that government shouldn't be held responsible for producing useful outcomes. According to their guiding Morality Play, "Government isn't smart enough to produce useful outcomes, so let's not even try."

Conservatives took from Grover Norquist the idea that taxes are always harmful and are always too high.

And they took from Newt Gingrich the idea that one doesn't have to use reason to justify one's agenda; one justifies the conservative agenda simply by waging non-stop propaganda wars against liberals. So much for, "I yield to the gentleman for whom I have the utmost degree of respect," or similar shows of courtesy among Americans of different views.

And, in one of history's perverse contradictions, America's conservatives have fulfilled Friedrich Hayek's darkest prophecy. Let ideologues win power, Hayek had warned, and they will govern in an ideology-first manner, ignoring the cause-and-effect realities of the nation they were elected to serve. When he first made this point, it was meant as a warning against the election of socialist ideologues. In the end, though,

Hayek's warning has turned into a forecast of how easy it is for conservative ideologues to go astray once they take office.

Conservatism is noteworthy for the addictive power of its Morality Play loyalties. Conservatives don't encourage their followers to see the world in an open-minded way; cause-and-effect reasoning has been tossed aside in favor of Morality Play loyalties. It is unsettling to see so many of our fellow Americans lose their bearings so enthusiastically.

But we will not win our conservative friends to a more sensible form of Americanism by asking them to be liberals. If America is to work properly, both parties will need to reinvent themselves as parties that put the public interest first and their own ideologies second. Both parties will have to reinvent themselves as parties with a dedication to Character and Craftsmanship. Such reinvention won't be easy for anyone – liberals will struggle with it, and conservatives will struggle even more.

Remember the truism I offered at the beginning? *Bad systems make good people do bad things.* Modern-day conservatism has given this truism an especially sharp and dangerous edge.

Time for a Remedial Lesson in the Role of Political Narratives

Watch a political debate and what will you see? You will see Republican candidates marketing themselves with a conservative narrative about how America is supposed to work, how it has gotten badly off track, and how they can fix it. You will see Democratic candidates marketing themselves with liberal or progressive narratives about how America is supposed to work and how they will get it back on track.

The candidates will talk past each other because we have lost track of what it is that a political narrative is supposed to do for us. Is it meant to teach? Or is limited to name-calling?

In a nation of Character and Craftsmanship, a wise political narrative will sum up the nation's challenges and it will recommend reforms that have some chance of success.

In a stuck America, our parties create static narratives that reaffirm unchanging Morality Play narratives. The point is not to help America overcome its difficulties, the point is to use potent emotional symbols in hopes of capturing as many votes as possible.

In an unstuck America, our parties would use the process of creating political narratives in a more adult and forward-looking way. They would appreciate the seriousness of America's challenges, and they would put together narratives based on Character and Craftsmanship in hopes of working out better choices for the future.

It's a huge difference. In today's immature partisan climate, a party's core narrative celebrates its core values, no matter how much stuckness those values produce. Put ideologues in power, as Hayek warned, and you'll find yourselves getting stuck. Today's narratives rationalize yesterday's subpar decisions. They don't point us toward real solutions.

In a mature America, parties would pay attention to Character and Craftsmanship in the shaping of their narratives and there'd be a real prospect for progress in what the parties promised the nation. Neither party would stay with the same narrative from one election to the next to the next. Both parties would have narratives that acknowledge America's stuckness; both parties would have narratives that describe the shifts by which they hope to see America get unstuck.

We have wholly forgotten the central importance of wise narratives in helping America find its way forward. Good narratives establish our priorities. Wise lawmakers work with those priorities and insist on finding responsible cause-and-effect solutions. A wise nation would use its political narratives to pull together the fruits of its cause-and-effect evaluations; both parties would develop narratives aimed at making America truly wiser and healthier.

In other words, the purpose of a wise narrative is to help candidates explain to voters our Three-Sixty responsibilities. What sort of capitalist economy is truly in the best interests of the American people and the nation as a whole? What sort of labor market is best for America? How much of America's rising prosperity ought to go for rising wages at the bottom? How much ought to go to the enrichment of those at the very top? How are America's environmental challenges to be responsibly addressed? How are the flaws of America's ghettoized cities to be overcome?

Wise narratives are necessarily rooted in rigorous cause-and-effect thinking. Let's say that your favorite candidate subscribes to the idea that America's medical sector has been functioning as a remorseless cartel. It wouldn't be enough to complain. You'd want the candidate to advance a promising way of overcoming this behavior and replacing it with something much safer.

Nor would it be enough for a candidate to say "We need to reduce carbon dioxide *emissions*," and stop there. Reduce emissions how? Over what kind of timetable? With what benefit in the long run? A candidate who's gotten to the bottom of the issue would argue for a comprehensive switch to clean energy technologies. She would argue for a lasting halt to the rise in carbon dioxide.

A civic ethos of Character and Craftsmanship is essential for both our political parties; it's the only ethos by which we prevent both parties from deceiving themselves about America's stuckness and therefore attempting to deceive the rest of us as well. Guiding narratives rooted in traditions of Character and Craftsmanship need to become the expected standard for all Republicans, and for all Democrats, and for all of us as grassroots citizens.

In today's America, the frozen narratives of the Right and the frozen narratives of the Left play into our nation's stuckness. In our hearts, we all know this. It's time to break ourselves free.

It's not easy to create cause-and-effect systems that truly serve the national interest. Today's ideologues get in the way. It's time to hold both parties and all candidates to a higher standard. The hero's journey ahead begins with the shedding of false certainties. It becomes a journey of looking for voices that truly deserve our trust.

With **political realignment**
came intensified division.

Both parties *left behind*
their one-time concern
for the national interest.

Both parties *gave themselves*
over to partisan warfare.

Getting America **UnStuck**
The Politics of **Character** & **Craftsmanship**

americaunstuck.com

Chapter Four

Craftsmanship
THE CUMMINS EXAMPLE

"Aiming for ten thousand times fewer defects."

LET'S BEGIN WITH A CRAFTSMANSHIP SUCCESS STORY, one that unfolds across four chapters. Cummins is a diesel engine manufacturing company that operates worldwide. In the first chapter of this story, 1983-1984, I was a new-hire out of business school, a "team adviser" on the assembly line at the Jamestown Engine Plant at the far western edge of New York State. Those were still the days of traditional manufacturing – inadequate quality standards, bulging inventories, and manufacturing rhythms that were anything but smooth.

In the second chapter, 1984 – 1985, I headed a small team at JEP loosely charged with figuring out what Komatsu knew about manufacturing that was still beyond Cummins' reach, and, more specifically, with figuring out what that might mean for the Jamestown Engine Plant.

In the third chapter – a period in which my wife and I no longer worked at Cummins – the company had taken on the challenge of achieving Six Sigma manufacturing and urged its entire supply chain to join the company in its Six Sigma quest.

In the fourth chapter, in 2007, my wife and I returned for a tour of the Jamestown Engine Plant after a twenty-two year absence and witnessed a dramatically improved manufacturing environment. What we had scented in the early 1980s as only a gentle whiff had taken hold and transformed both the company and its suppliers.

The arc of the Cummins story begins with a tradition-bound culture and ends with transformational success.

It's a success story whose dominant themes speak of high standards, transformational ambitions, and persistent, step-by-step improvements. One can read it as a triumph of Character and Craftsmanship.

One can also read it as a lesson about imitation. What if Cummins' rivals hadn't already set a higher standard for it to imitate? Would it have pursued its transformational agenda with the same tenacity? No one can say for sure, but it seems unlikely. Competitive pressure had a lot to do with Cummins willingness to transform.

Also included in the larger lesson of success is a cautionary tale about a labor union that couldn't adapt.

It's a modern morality tale. In the first chapter of the Cummins story, those immersed in the manufacturing culture of the day grumbled constantly about fate and the endless struggle of keeping the assembly line on schedule even though shipments of faulty parts were unavoidable and endlessly disruptive. All it takes is a bad batch of a single component – sometimes as simple as a washer – and all the engines that contain the faulty component would end up being taken apart so that the faulty component could be swapped out for properly made replacements. Think of the assembly line running backwards. Think of hours and hours of overtime, everyone frantic beyond measure. The chronic headache of unreliable quality hit the line again, and again, and again. Chapter One was a chapter of chronic pain. The engines were excellent – if the parts that went into them were well-made. But not otherwise.

In the second chapter, the story line begins to change. We began to visualize the world of manufacturing as a world of manageable variables. Sometimes all the crucial variables behave themselves and things go well; sometimes the variables misbehave, and things go badly. But in principle, so the new thinking held, all those variables could be *understood*. And, with enough persistence, they could also be *controlled*.

Does a drill bit work well for the first thousand holes it cuts? And then does it begin to wear down to the point where it no longer cuts accurately? There is a discoverable cause-and-effect relationship at work, but to learn what that relationship is, one must make a practice of observing and measuring all the relevant variables. One develops a hypothesis – "wear is a function of total service cycles." One tracks the time and date at which the drill is placed in service. One tracks its service cycles. One measures its ability to stay within spec. And in time one learns just how long the drill bit can be trusted to work properly. One puts a new procedure in place. Drill bits are to be replaced after X cycles of use.

Worn drill bits no longer become a source of poor quality, because the rules of the manufacturing system no longer permit them to stay in service longer than they should.

And so on, through one process variable after another, after another.

The same principle applies to the assembly line. Picture in your mind an upside down engine block. A new crankshaft has been lowered into place. Six sets of pistons need to be fastened to the crankshaft with six pairs of capscrews (i.e. bolts) installed and tightened. The assembler working this station has an air-powered impact wrench. *Zzzp, zzzp. Zzzp, zzzp. Zzzp, zzzp. Zzzp, zzzp. Zzzp, zzzp. Zzzp, zzzp.* Twelve capscrews. Twelve blasts with the impact wrench.

Do this all day long. Twelve times per crankshaft. Two hundred crankshafts per shift. Is it possible that you might someday lose count? Maybe you'll be distracted by the need to sneeze. Or by a funny story someone wants to share. Or by worry about your shopping list. Who knows?

The level of attention you give to each engine will vary, will it not? In other words, the amount of attention you pay is a variable. And what if you miss a capscrew, and send just one engine down the line with one capscrew that isn't properly tightened? When the engine is fired up in the test cell, the piston that's not properly attached to the crankshaft will come loose and blow a huge hole in the side of the engine block. If the tech who's working the test cell happens to be standing in the wrong place, she'll be killed.

So how does a factory manage this variable properly? So that every piston will be properly tightened, every time, several thousand times a month, month after month after month? The plant's manufacturing engineers will "idiot-proof" the workstation. They'll attach an automatic counter to the impact wrench. Every time the team member working that station releases the engine, the counter will run a safety check. Did the impact wrench actually tighten twelve capscrews? If Yes, the engine will be released and will move to its next workstation. If No, alarms will sound, lights will flash, and the team member who missed a capscrew will have to tighten all capscrews again just to be sure.

This isn't the only way to idiot-proof that particular operation, of course, but I cite it to make the larger point. *Every* variable that affects the quality of a manufacturing process has to be identified, studied, understood, and managed. And that's essentially the journey that Cummins took on. If it was to defend its position as one of the world's leading diesel engine manufacturers, it would have to bring every variable under control. Every time.

In the previous chapter of this story, no one would have believed it possible. Understand every variable? Learn how to manage every variable so that it *always* produces the desired results? What a dream!

But since some of Cummins' competitors had already made that journey, Cummins had little choice.

And so that's the second chapter of the Cummins story. The light went on. There's a transformational alternative to the old way of running a manufacturing company. Why not seize it? Cummins put itself on a transformational path.

It's not easy to appreciate just what a stretch this would have to be. The jargon of Three Sigma and Six Sigma sounds quite simple. The reality behind those two terms is quite extraordinary. Three Sigma quality – the quality standard that typified traditional factories – implied a defect rate of only two parts per hundred. Six Sigma quality – the standard Cummins now follows – implies a defect rate of only two parts per million.

Let's use the same denominator for both those terms – let's state them both in defects per million. Three Sigma quality implies *twenty thousand* defects per million. Six Sigma quality implies only *two* defects per million.

That's right. JEP's acceptable defect rate is ten thousand times lower than it used to be. (Technically, one-ten thousandth of what it used to be.)

It was a long journey, for Cummins and all of its suppliers, to incorporate a Six Sigma way of life into how their machining lines and assembly lines were to operate.

And that was the Third Chapter. Cummins and its suppliers jointly had to make the journey to a Six Sigma future. It took years of effort to unlearn the old ways and internalize the new ways of doing business.

In the fourth chapter, the vision has been achieved. Once the quality of every single component can be trusted, life on the assembly line loses its jerky, stop-start rhythm. Parts flow smoothly from the suppliers to the line. And the line flows smoothly, because the risk of failure has been removed at every step along the way.

In the early 1980s, when my wife and I worked at JEP, its Assembly & Test business unit must have had two thousand linear feet of shelving, devoted to storing an endless inventory of assembly line parts. When we toured the assembly line in 2007, the difference was striking. The storage shelving had disappeared! Boxes of parts came off their delivery trucks and were moved directly to the line. If you don't need inventory, you don't need inventory shelves and you don't need lots of fork lift guys moving inventory around.

In 1985, the assembly line produced 50 engines a day on one shift. In 2007, JEPs assembly line produced 475 engines a day across two shifts.

Not all those who worked for Cummins were able to accept the company's journey of reinvention. At Plant One in Columbus, Indiana, the diesel workers' union was thrown off by the challenge of Continuous Improvement.

Old-fashioned unionism had been stamped by the habits of a very different era. Labor-management contracts from an earlier era had been shaped by the idea that factory jobs were essentially unchanging and that it made sense for union members to feel that their contracts gave them property rights in their jobs. Jobs were done the same way, year in and year out, and from time to time a person's seniority allowed him to advance to a new job that paid a little bit more. It was no accident that jobs felt like entitlements; every single position in a factory's pecking order had been sanctified by contract and by the weight of history.

By the 1980s, though, all this had begun to break down. Global competition was pushing everyone into a different era, an era of frequent job redesign. This was such a difficult break with tradition that some unionized shops couldn't handle it, and, alas, the union at Plant One was among them. After a long and unsuccessful effort to win over the union to a spirit of continuous improvement, senior management said, "Enough," and transferred Plant One's product line from Columbus to Jamestown. Employees at Jamestown ended up with 11-liter and 15-liter engines on their assembly line; at Plant One the assembly line went dark.

America needs unions, but not at the expense of permanent industrial backwardness. Unions that welcome a spirit of permanent improvement can play a vital role in America's future; unions that cannot imagine themselves as partners in continuous improvement won't have nearly the role they used to have.

Why is the Cummins' example important?

Cummins had enough character to raise its standards to near-perfect levels. Cummins had enough imagination to visualize a transformational outcome.

And Cummins had the persistence to keep moving forward, in partnership with its suppliers, to higher and higher levels of performance. In time, Cummins and its suppliers achieved the transformational outcome they had sought.

Think Character – in the form of very high standards. Think Craftsmanship – in the journey of its entire supply chain to an extraordinary level of professionalism.

It's an apt lesson for the American people. As with Cummins, America's long-run success also depends on our Character and our Craftsmanship. As with Cummins, America's long-run success will also depend on our willingness to accept transformational goals.

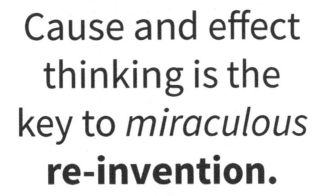

Cause and effect thinking is the key to *miraculous* **re-invention.**

★

Chapter Five

Craftsmanship
THE SCHOOL REFORM EXAMPLE

"Teasing out the difference between reform and transformation."

THERE'S BEEN QUITE A BIT OF DEBATE in America about school reform, a debate that's lively as ever.

And in this chapter, I will paint our choice in broad terms. Will those in charge of our schools perpetuate a long-standing tradition of incremental thinking and incremental adjustents? Or will our entire nation finally take note of those who have been transformational leaders? Will our entire nation step up and learn from its most far-sighted educators and its most successful schools?

Before I go further down this path, I want to take note of an educational nonprofit that I used to work for, Education Resource Strategies, which works quietly with individual school systems, helping first one set of leaders and then another to rethink the cause-and-effect links between how they allocate resources and the learning gains their children experience.

Karen Hawley Miles and Stephen Frank and the rest of the ERS team have helped dozens and dozens of school systems rise to the challenge of managing their resources in smarter and more focused ways. ERS pays careful attention to district-by-district specifics. Help leaders size up their particular context. Help them do their fine-tuning more wisely, and their systems will become stronger and their children will make stronger gains.

ERS renders an important service. But is this approach to incremental improvement, solid as it is, the last and best word in school system improvement? I'm not convinced. I salute ERS, the skills it develops, and the gains it stimulates.

At the same time, one also sees schools that take a more transformational approach, and help their students achieve even stronger gains.

It's important for us as a nation to wrap our minds around the choices that have been put before us.

As we know, there is something of a school reform debate under way on the national stage, with three different sets contending voices. None of these are the voices of transformation; all are voices of incremental reform. The nation's most transformational leaders have been left on the sidelines of this debate, in part because they don't fit neatly into anyone's ideological box. Their idiosyncratic genius plays a large role in their exceptional success with their pupils, but it also leaves them somewhat sidelined whenever the national stage is claimed by folks with much simpler answers.

The simple way to frame the distinction between reformers and transformational leaders is to note that reformers take a "What's Broken?" approach to school improvement; transformational leaders take a "What's Missing?" approach.

Those who ask "What's Broken?" hope to improve the nation's schools by finding better ways to manage the grownups who run them. I have written this chapter partly as a cautionary tale about the insufficient Craftsmanship on the part of America's established school systems, and partly as an invitation to investigate more fully the successes of those leaders who have demonstrated much higher levels of Craftsmanship in how they put schools together. If those who ask "What's Broken?" end up with new ways to "manage the grownups," those who ask "What's Missing?" are more likely to end up with new ways of engaging their students.

This distinction is crucial to the journey of Character and Craftsmanship that lies ahead.

If by "Craftsmanship" one means working within an existing paradigm and settling for incremental adjustments, it is not likely that America will get the best out of its schools. And yet the entire momentum of American public education is shaped by powerful forces of incrementalism, from the bureaucratic traditions of school system leaders, to the bureaucratic traditions of teachers, to the incremental instincts of parents. How could America's schools not bear the imprint of incrementalism?

And yet having the deck stacked in favor of incremental change isn't necessarily in America's best interests.

In the last chapter, as you will recall, a manufacturing company that didn't want to be left behind was forced to learn a new way of thinking and a new way of managing its production activities. A world class standard already existed; its value in the marketplace had been proven, so those who wanted to stay in business found themselves in a game of catch up.

In public education, the challenge is more complex. Students from different backgrounds might well benefit from different kinds of schools. A school whose methods excel with upper middle class children may not be relevant to the children of poverty. Schools that excel in educating children of poverty may not be relevant to the needs of upper middle class children.

Yet by themselves these disparities don't account for the flat-footed nature of the present debate.

Up till now, what's been at stake has not been so much the educational future of America's children as the cultures of conformity among the grown-ups.

Most of those who come to the policy debate on public education bring with them the same unstated premise. The way to improve America's schools is for the nation to do a better job of managing the grownups who run them. Democrats make this error; Republicans make this error.

One faction has provoked an intense quarrel over the nation's curriculum standards. Shall we have a common core curriculum? It's an important question, but please note its starting assumption: If only the relevant grownups can be induced to accept a better curriculum, the nation's children will automatically benefit.

There's another faction that's passionately in favor of charter schools. They surmise that America's schools would be better if they were stimulated by a spirit of competition. Create charter schools, they say, and we will have the competition our schools need. It's an interesting argument, but note again the starting assumption: If only the grownups were exposed to more competition, they'd become better teachers.

In yet another debate, communities have mobilized to insist on local control of schools. Is that our best path forward? Shall we insist on giving local authorities complete control over their schools? This, too is an important question, but note again the starting assumption. Success for our schools will be determined by the nation's choice of rules about which set of grownups are to be put in charge.

Note the failing that's common to all three debates. All of them revolve around the privileges and duties of various sets of grownups; none begin with children and the question of who has already had the greatest success in educating children.

In other words, no one asks, "What's missing?" from the schools we create for children. All three arguments begin with their proponents claiming to have the nation's smartest answers to the "What's broken?" question. What's broken is the curriculum. What's broken is the lack of competition. What's broken is the loss of local control. And from those assertions they jump immediately to their own fixes.

It's not the best way for the American people to bring this matter into focus, but it does seem to be our reflexive response.

Their fixes are based on their values. One faction values curriculum thoroughness; one faction values competition; one faction values local control. But none of these factions have all that much to say about the deeper question of Responsibility. What does it take for all schools to fulfill their Responsibility to educate children?

Ask about Responsibility and we shall then be called upon to ask "What's Missing?" in the way schools go about educating children. The thinking process will then go something like this.

"Aren't we responsible for educating *all* the children? Of course we are. That's the standard we want to meet. But what if we haven't figured out all the success factors that are crucial to reaching all children and educating all children?"

This sort of curiosity would take us in a promising direction. We might find ourselves asking, "What's it take to engage children – *all children* – and inspire them to learn?" We might find ourselves asking, *"What's missing* in our public schools? What are the success factors that – if present – would inspire *all* our children to learn?"

Such questions could open the door to a more transformational spirit. That shouldn't be a bad thing, should it? Our traditions of incremental reform haven't been enough, have they? Isn't it possible that a spirit of openness to transformational thinking will be America's better choice?

Back in the 1990s, as my kids were going through public schools in the Annapolis area, I couldn't help but notice our county's high dropout rate. Anne Arundel County schools might have 5,000 eighth graders one year, and then 4,000 twelfth graders four years later – implying a rough dropout rate of twenty percent. And yet, despite these year after year failure indications, our school system persistently reported a four percent dropout rate.

That sort of dishonesty was eventually overturned by No Child Left Behind, but until Congress acted, school systems across America made a fetish of understating their true dropout rates.

In any event, irked by our school district's evident commitment to a culture of mediocrity, I began to pay attention to those principals who had success stories to tell, especially those in schools that serve children of poverty. In time, I had heard enough different speeches, and read enough different accounts of remarkable schools, that I began to sense a unifying pattern to the success stories of the nation's very best principals.

I won't say they asked, "What's it take to achieve six sigma success in an elementary school?" They didn't. Nor had they asked themselves, "What would Komatsu do?"

Clearly, though, they had all pushed themselves to find solid strategies for succeeding with every child. They had moved beyond asking, "What's Broken?" and had with a relish taken on the question, "What's Missing?"

Quite obviously our most talented leaders had asked themselves, "What activities must to be present in a school if every child is to engage, if every child is to succeed?" And they hadn't let matters rest till they had developed approaches they trusted.

And from their wide-ranging willingness to tinker with all parts of the process, the nation's most successful principals and teachers had developed similar implicit hypotheses about what it takes for every child to learn. Mike Feinberg and Dave Levin of the Knowledge Is Power Program, or KIPP, are surely the most visible.[1] As I write, the KIPP website speaks of at least 180 KIPP schools in operation across America.

If I may generalize, partly from KIPP's successes, and partly from the successes of other dedicated principals and teachers, I think it's fair to say that principals at the nation's very best schools are obsessed with four essentials:

---

1 - See, for example, Jay Matthews. *Work Hard, Be Nice. How Two Inspired Teachers Created the Most Promising Schools in America.* Algonquin Books of Chapel Hill. 2009.

First, every child has to feel connected; every child has to feel motivated.

Second, every lesson has to be learnable, for every child.

Third, every teacher has to be good at giving on-target coaching to every child.

Fourth, every child has to work hard enough, every week, to learn every lesson well. One might call it "learning to mastery."

Four central hypotheses, guidelines to the sort of processes their schools would have to develop. Four ways of asking "What's Missing?" and doing their very best to accumulate the best possible answers.

Taken together, these four hypotheses form a coherent success hypothesis:

> *A child will become a successful student when he or she is connected and motivated, when he or she can understand and absorb every lesson, when he or she receives spot-on coaching every time something seems confusing, and when he or she works hard enough, each week, to learn all the material.*

Create schools capable of meeting these standards for every child, and they will regularly outperform schools run by those who emphasize the importance of managing the grownups better.

Toyota had looked at its machining and assembly operations and had asked itself, "What's it take to succeed *every single time?*" By asking itself this question with enough intensity, it slowly weaned itself out of the chronic failure business and learned how to put itself into the repeatable success business.

Taken as a whole, the nation's public school systems have yet to take that step. They haven't been led by people willing to set aside their old rule books and ask themselves the harder, better question: "What's it take to succeed with *every* child? *Every* day? In *every* lesson?"

Yet in small corners of American society, there are great principals who have done exactly that.

They've gotten away from asking, "What's broken?" and have taught themselves to ask, "What's missing?" They've gotten away from asking, "How do we get every kid to obey?" and switched to asking, "How do we get every kid to engage so intensely that every kid learns?"

They've gotten away from asking, "How do we do a better job of managing our teachers," to asking, "How do we do a great job of inspiring and engaging every single one of our children?"

They've gotten away from being cautious incrementalists.

They aspired to something more, much more. And in their courage they have created transformational success stories.

How might our nation take advantage of what these innovators have already achieved?

Let's give ourselves permission to think about our schools with the same transformational spirit already shown by America's best principals and teachers.

Let's set aside the entire crowd of politicized grownups who want to turn schools into laboratories for someone's Perfect Curriculum or someone else's Perfect Charter School or someone else's Perfect Example of Local Control. There are so many ax-grinding ways to ask, "What's Broken?" and none of them lead us toward transformational change.

Let's turn instead to the principals who've produced real successes and ask them to share their stories. Let's acknowledge the special people who have shown the way and learn all we can from them.

And once we've soaked up what they have to say, let's invite the nation's teachers to brainstorm with one another about how best to take advantage of those lessons in the schools where they work.

Let's have district by district brainstorming exercises.

Let's invite teachers within each district – and beyond, if they like – to imagine schools so engaging that *every* child feels cared about, so appealing that every child connects. It's an ancient truth – children learn faster when they feel loved.

Let's invite them to describe their ideas of what it would mean to have every lesson be truly learnable. For every child.

Let's invite brainstorming on what it takes for teachers to develop the art of spot-on coaching.

Let's invite brainstorming on what it would take for kids to learn every lesson to mastery.

No one starts from zero. Almost everyone in teaching will have creative suggestions to offer. Let's pose these questions to our teachers and then listen respectfully to the ideas they generate.

Are those four questions enough? Perhaps there are more we would want to ask. Here in Anne Arundel County our current superintendent wants to identify every infant with learning issues, at the earliest possible opportunity, in order to provide the parents and the child with in-home coaching, so that the children can be brought along from the outset. A well-coached child will have a much easier time taking hold once she starts pre-kindergarten. Early intervention can head off greater difficulties later.

It's a great question. "How do we make sure every child arrives at school as ready to learn as possible?" Here, too, one senses the importance of focusing on children and how they learn.

A nation working from within its own spirit of wellness won't mind taking transformational approaches to difficult challenges. Public schools in a healthy and self-confident democracy will get themselves past "What's Broken?" and will turn themselves, mind and heart, to the challenge of figuring out "What's Missing?"

It's okay to set high standards. We want the business models for public education to be so effective that America fulfills its larger responsibilities to all the nation's children, not just those who live in good neighborhoods.

It's a mark of good character to want every school to work well for the children it serves. And it's a mark of good craftsmanship to give ourselves permission to think transformationally about the journey toward full educational success.

Asking **"What's broken?"**
has never been the best way
to create *great* schools.

America's best educators start
by asking **"What's missing?"**
and they don't rest till they've
created schools that *engage*
and *educate* every child.

Chapter Six

Craftsmanship
THE INEQUALITY EXAMPLE

"The Federal Government changed sides."

THERE'S A GENERAL AGREEMENT TODAY that economic inequality is real, that it's getting worse, and that action might be needed. In spite of America's gains on social issues, working Americans have taken heavy losses on the economic front.

In Chapter 1, I offered a graph showing that the income shares going to the Bottom 90%, the Next 9%, and the Top 1% have changed dramatically since the late 1970s. Once it was a 68/23/9 split. Now it's a 52/30/18 split.

There has been so much upward redistribution of income since then that those in the Bottom 90% have seen their share of the nation's economic pie shrink by more than a fifth.

Now let's view this same story from a slightly different angle. I use the same database but I ask a different question. For each presidency, how were the gains of that presidency split between the same three income groups? How much of the new income generated during Truman's time in office went to those in the Bottom 90%? How much of the gain went to the Next 9%? How much to the Top 1%?

As it happens, during the Truman years the new earnings were divided as follows: Sixty-seven percent of the economy's new pretax earnings went to those in the Bottom 90%. Twenty-two percent of the new earnings went to the Next 9%. Eleven percent of the new earnings went to the Top 1%.

And so it went, from one Administration to the next, with roughly the same division each time, until the Reagan years, when the American economy made an abrupt shift. Only forty-one percent of the economy's gains went to Americans in the Bottom 90%. Those in the Next 9% captured thirty percent of the economy's gains. Those in the Top 1% saw their share of the economy's new gains shoot up to 29%.

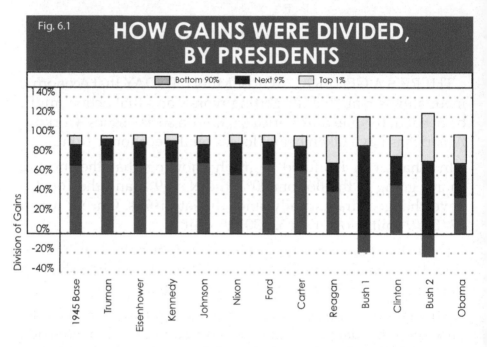

Figure 6.1. Saez op cit. Author's calculations from Saez database.

Let's pause for a moment while I explain how I put this analysis together.

I followed the practice of David Bartels in assigning the first year of each new presidency to the economic record of the former president. Eisenhower's first year is treated as part of Truman's presidency; Kennedy's first year is treated as part of Eisenhower's presidency, and so on.

In two instances, the presidencies of Bush 1 and Bush 2, Americans in the Bottom 90% found themselves earning less money at the end of the two Bush presidencies than they had at the beginning. In other words, since they had received a negative share of the economy's gains, their piece of the bar chart had to fall below the 0% line. Meanwhile, the gross proceeds of the other two groups had to total more than 100%.

Think of the gains as having been distributed this way: The Bottom 90 took a 20% loss. The Next 9 captured 90% of the economy's new earnings. And the Top 1 captured 30% of the economy's new earnings. Add these results together: A twenty percent loss, a ninety percent gain, a thirty percent gain. Together these three parts add up to 100% of the economy's new earnings.

Now step back and take in the broad pattern, beginning with the Truman presidency and extending to the early years of the Obama presidency. From the "1945 Base" (the first bar) through the first seven postwar presidencies, there's not a lot of shifting going on. In each of these presidencies, those in the Bottom 90% capture at least sixty percent of the economy's new earnings. In one case, those in the bottom tier capture seventy-three percent of the economy's new earnings.

Meanwhile, those in the Top 1% capture anywhere from two percent to eleven percent of the economy's new earnings. And so on.

Then an abrupt change takes place. In the Reagan years, and in the four presidencies since Reagan, the share of our economy's new pretax earnings received by the Bottom 90% takes a sharp plunge. The economy's new pretax earnings are overwhelmingly diverted to those in the Next 9% and the Top 1%.

This isn't something that crept up on the American economy over a stretch of several presidential administrations, as the globalization hypothesis might imply. Instead, it arrived as a hammer blow during the Reagan years, and this abrupt shift of fortunes has been America's norm ever since.

But what is one to make of the causes? And where might we turn for the cures? As a society, our thinking about inequality and where it came from has been remarkably fuzzy.

Interpreting the Shift

Some have diagnosed the declining fortunes of working Americans as the inevitable consequences of an increasingly high tech era. Today's jobs require greater skills, or so it is said, and American workers who haven't improved their skills will inevitably fall behind.

Others have diagnosed the pain being felt at the bottom of the workforce as the fruit of a shrinking manufacturing sector. It's not that there aren't good jobs in this economy; there just aren't nearly as many as there used to be.

Or the jobs still exist, but regrettably they've gone overseas.

In any event, we are told, the inequality that working Americans now experience is largely the product of forces beyond anyone's control.

And since these trends supposedly took hold over time, if the situation is to be treated at all, the proper treatments will have to take hold gradually as well. Let's do a better job of workforce training, but let's not expect remarkable results. Let's modify tax policies, in hopes of curbing capital flight, but let's not expect inequality to change that much. Let's raise the minimum wage a bit, but not too much, and let's not expect a significant impact. And so on.

All these measures taken together are thought to be steps in the right direction. Each is needed, but there's no magic in any of them. Today's new economy simply isn't as kind to American working people as the old economy used to be.

That's been the story line offered by mainstream pundits for quite some time. Is it on the mark? A number of observers have argued that if these trends were the real cause, then they'd have produced the same results in other industrialized nations too.

But that hasn't been the case. Only in America has the top ten percent wrung as much wealth from the rest of the population; only in America has the workforce taken it on the chin so badly.[1]

To my mind, the "Inequality" story line badly misrepresents what really happened. FDR had created an economy in which the fruits of America's rising productivity were broadly shared. The American Dream worked for everyone.

Then the Federal Government changed sides. Reagan's economic program killed the American Dream for tens of millions in the middle class and below, so that most of the economy's rising wealth could be diverted to those at the very top, with the Top One Percent benefiting the most. It wasn't globalization that created this shift; the Reagan Administration created this shift, and too many of the nation's Democrats played along. The nation's capitalist elites used globalization as an excuse for upward redistribution, and as a fig leaf for hiding the real causes. Globalization became a handy tool for amplifying wage cuts at the bottom and explosive compensation gains at the top. It wasn't the central cause, but its amplifying effects were welcomed by America's newly enriched elites.

Even without globalization, the Reagan Revolution would have sought and achieved the same end. It would still have moved all the benefits of America's rising productivity to those at the top. It would still have killed the American Dream for those at the bottom.

Here I will look at two versions of what is essentially the same story – the Emmanuel Saez version and the Stephen J. Rose version. Saez is an economist at the University of California, Berkeley, as mentioned already. Stephen J. Rose is an economist associated with the Urban Institute in Washington, D.C.

---

1 - Thomas Piketty. *Capital in the Twenty-First Century.* Harvard. 2014.
See, for example, his charts on pages 323 and 324, showing much higher gains for the top ten percent in the U.S.

Saez works with IRS data. Rose works with data from the Current Population Survey, as compiled by the U.S. Census Department. Saez adjusts for inflation over time using the Consumer Price Index (CPI). Rose adjusts for inflation over time using the Personal Consumption Expenditure (PCE) price deflator. In comparing the two, I would guess that the PCE helps us tell the overall story with just a bit more realism than the CPI. Saez data, as adjusted inflation using the CPI, make total growth for working Americans look just a bit more bleak than seems reasonable.

Let's start with the picture that sits quietly within the Saez database. Figure 6.2 tells the story in just a few simple numbers.

Let's begin with the postwar years, 1945-1981, when the economy operated under what I have called "FDR's Rules." During that period, average earnings for those in the Bottom 90% rise by 77%. Average earnings for the Next 9% rise by 103%. Average earnings for the Top 1% rise by 29%. Extraordinary, isn't it? Earnings growth for those in the Bottom 90% outpaces earnings growth for the Top 1%!

Then everything flips. The next column, 1981 – 2007, takes us from the beginning of the Reagan years to the eve of the Crash in 2008. For those in the Bottom 90%, average earnings are only 8% higher in 2007 than they had been in 1981. For those in the Next 9%, earnings over the same period rise by 48%. And for those in the Top 1%, average earnings are 206% higher in 2007!

The third column tells the same story, but takes it through the Crash of 2008 and on into 2014. The Bottom 90% are worse off in 2014 than they were in 1981. The Next 9% are still 48% better off. The Top 1% isn't 206% better off any longer, it's only (only!) 176% better off.

Stephen Rose finds much the same broader pattern of outcomes, though his approach to calculating inflation softens the story just a bit. Here's what he says: "In 1979, the bottom three income groups (lower class, lower middle class, and middle class) controlled 70 percent of all incomes, and the

Fig. 6.2 REAL EARNING GAINS BY GROUP AND PERIOD			
Earnings Group	1945 - 1981	1981 - 2007	1981 - 2014
Bottom 90%	77%	8%	-3%
Next 9%	103%	48%	48%
Top 1%	29%	206%	176%

Figure 6.2 Saez op cit. Author's calculations. Table repeats data from Introduction.

upper middle class and rich controlled 30 percent. By 2014, this distribution shifted to 37 percent for the bottom three groups and 63 percent for the upper middle class and rich groups."[2]

Suppose we were to apply the PCE inflation deflator to the Saez data. How would the numbers change for the 1981 – 2007 period? They'd be softened, just a bit. Incomes for the Bottom 90% would be up by 17%, rather than 8%. Incomes for the Next 9% would be up 60% rather than 48%. Incomes for the Top 1% would be up 231% rather than 206%. The picture isn't as stark for the Bottom 90% as the Saez data suggests. With a more realistic inflation adjustment, its character softens – just slightly. Still, the contrast between how the economy functioned for working Americans in the pre-Reagan years and how it has functioned for working Americans since then is stunning – and brutal.

Saez' database forces me to draw a hard line at the 90% mark. Above that mark, the privileged ten percent. Below that mark, the exploited ninety percent. While it draws a useful contrast,

---

2 - Stephen J. Rose. *The Growing Size and Incomes of the Upper Middle Class.* The Urban Institute. June 2016. P. 14.

I find myself a bit more comfortable with the picture that Rose has constructed. Drawing the line at 90% probably isn't the choice we'd want to make if the Saez database were more detailed. We'd probably agree with Rose that the upper middle class is growing – he puts the upper middle class and the upper class at just over thirty percent of the whole. And we'd focus our concern not on the "Bottom 90%" as I do here, but on the Bottom 70%.

Still, both the Saez approach and the Rose approach concur on the central point of this chapter – a striking redistribution of earnings got under way at the beginning of the Reagan years. The share of the nation's earnings going to those in the bottom two-thirds of the economy has shrunk; the share going to those in the upper third has increased; the increase going to those at the top has increased the most.

It's at the very top where the Saez database gives us a far sharper picture of what's happening than Rose can manage from within the limitations of his dataset. Rose relies on survey data from the Census, a methodology that will never clarify the earnings of the super-rich as accurately as the IRS dataset.

Given the numbers, from Saez and also from Rose, what are we to conclude about the workings of the American economy? Are those in the Top One Percent getting richer by accident, while those in the Bottom Ninety Percent – or perhaps the Bottom Seventy Percent – lose ground as the result of anonymous economic forces?

As mentioned earlier, French economist Thomas Piketty uses cross-country comparisons to argue that inequality strains in the United States are largely self-inflicted. If we Americans were simply at the mercy of anonymous forces, then other advanced countries would have suffered from those same forces and would have similar inequality profiles. But American inequality is more intense, it turns out. Anonymous forces didn't do this to the American workforce. America's elites and their friends in Washington are the ones who pulled this off.

I think it's time we acknowledged that the shift documented here was the intended outcome of the Reagan Revolution. The federal government changed sides. And since it did, Americans at the top have been able to enrich themselves at a much higher rate of speed than before.

FDR's Rules had been designed to hold in check the appetites of the Top One Percent so that working Americans could participate fully in the nation's rising prosperity.

And Reagan's Rules were designed to reverse all this, to supercharge the enrichment of the Top One Percent by undercutting the bargaining power of working Americans.

The "Reagan Revolution," in other words, was really a counter-revolution. FDR's New Deal had created a Revolution, one that extended the fruits of American growth to Americans at all income levels. Reagan's Counter-Revolution was aimed at sweeping aside the entire apparatus of Prosperity Capitalism. Reagan's team was determined to restore the traditions of Enrichment Capitalism, as they had existed in America before the New Deal.

Globalization, then, hasn't been the anonymous and impersonal force so many pundits have claimed it was, causing a regrettable but unavoidable decline in jobs and earnings for millions of Americans. Quite the reverse. Globalization has been just another rationalization employed by the Top One Percent to weaken the earnings of working Americans in order to accelerate their own enrichment.

Fleshing Out the Story

Let's add some texture to these larger themes. And let's start with the New Deal years, when FDR was president, when America's manufacturing sector was on the rise and its unions had fought their way to the bargaining table. A new operating system took shape for the American economy, one that aimed at holding in check the greed of those that FDR referred to as "Economic Royalists." FDR's operating system held the Top

One Percent in check until Reagan became President.

These were the years of Prosperity Capitalism, the golden years for working Americans, and for its benefits the nation owed a large debt of gratitude to all those who helped President Roosevelt put together the New Deal economy that made them possible.

Prosperity Capitalism enjoyed a remarkable run, from the end of the Second World War all the way up to the beginning of the Reagan presidency.

And then, with Reagan in the White House and the nation's elites in control, Prosperity Capitalism was abruptly swept aside.

Four major shifts were involved in the switch from FDR's Rules to Reagan's Rules – changes in marginal tax rates, changes in Federal Reserve behavior, changes in the treatment of labor unions, and a ramping up of shareholder value ideology.[3]

Tax Rate Signals. Under the operating system for Prosperity Capitalism, marginal tax rates on the wealthiest Americans had been set at seventy percent and sometimes more – rates that survived from FDR's presidency on through Jimmy Carter's. Under Ronald Reagan, marginal tax rates were lowered first to fifty percent and then to twenty-eight percent. Of all the elements that make up the switch from Prosperity Capitalism to Enrichment Capitalism, this was probably the most consequential.

When marginal tax rates are high, they send the elites one

---

3 - This part of my argument isn't entirely original with me, but I must apologize to the reader. I cannot remember the author who highlighted marginal tax rates as the key to CEO behavior. And others before me have also noted the importance of the Federal Reserve's role and President Reagan's anti-union agenda. To their insights I add the notion of distinct operating systems and the two styles of capitalism they produce. I also add the emphasis on enrichment as an entitlement fed by the long stock market boom of the 1980s and 1990s.

kind of message. "America isn't meant to be an enrichment economy; it's meant to be a prosperity economy. The fruits of America's rising productivity are not to be monopolized by those at the top; the entire workforce is to benefit."

From a CEO's perspective, what's the point of raising one's salary when most of the raise will end up with Uncle Sam? High tax rates send a sharp message to those at the very top: Cool your jets! Moderate your appetites! The American economy has to work properly for everyone!

Conversely, when marginal tax rates are low, the nation's economic elites register a very different signal. "Things are different; the Federal Government has changed sides. It wants you to get rich. It doesn't care about the Bottom Seventy Percent. Raise your salaries, again and again, and you'll be allowed to keep most of the gains."

The result was predictable. Wage growth slowed to a crawl for lower income employees. Compensation growth for CEOs accelerated dramatically.

Federal Reserve Priorities. When Prosperity Capitalism was still America's norm, the Federal Reserve did its best to keep the economy at full employment. This fit right in with the needs of America's wage earners. Working Americans win raises more easily when the entire economy is operating at full employment. Working Americans had the Federal Reserve on their side during the era of Prosperity Capitalism.

But Prosperity Capitalism had a hidden weakness; it hadn't been designed to keep inflation in check. Every time the nation's labor unions negotiated contracts with cost-of-living raises, they inadvertently intensified the nation's inflationary weaknesses.

By the late 1970s, an inflationary spiral had taken hold in America, and as its severity intensified, the Federal Reserve had to switch its priorities. President Carter asked Paul Volcker to lead the Federal Reserve, and Volcker bravely raised interest rates, again and again, with the aim of slowing the economy enough to halt its inflationary spiral. It was a rough ride, but Volcker's medicine worked. The economy stalled; millions were thrown out of work; cost-of-living contracts disappeared. Inflation came skidding to a halt. And as the economy began to grow, everyone was relieved to see that inflation was no longer a threat.

But did the Federal Reserve then go back to promoting full employment? No. Paul Volcker's successor, Alan Greenspan, preferred to see the economy operating just a bit more slowly, with enough marginal unemployment to keep wages flattened and the threat of inflation quiescent. Greenspan's formula - chronic underemployment and flat wages – was understandably popular among employers. It's not what we need when Prosperity Capitalism is our aim, but it was warmly embraced as a central feature of the new era – the era of Enrichment Capitalism.

Suppression of Unionism. In the days of Prosperity Capitalism, the unionization rights of working Americans had been vigorously protected. That changed when Prosperity Capitalism was shut down and the economy was shunted onto the track of Enrichment Capitalism. FDR had protected America's unions; Reagan and his team were out to get rid of them.

The Ideology of Shareholder Value. Milton Friedman had already beaten the drum of shareholder value. CEOs weren't in the social betterment business, Friedman had argued, they were in the shareholder enrichment business. Friedmanism set the tone for what was to become the stock market orgy of the 1980s and 1990s. The era of shareholder enrichment had arrived, just as its leading apostle had wanted it to.

With the wages of working Americans flattened, corporate profits and CEO compensation levels climbed. And climbed.

For those in the Top One Percent, the Rapture had arrived.

But working Americans? They became this nation's Left Behind.

The stock market finally peaked in early 2000, but not until its long rise had ignited an ideology of endless enrichment for those at the very top.

At the highest reaches of American capitalism, a CEO subtext had taken hold: "We CEOs are entitled to enrich ourselves at speeds far faster than the speed of GDP growth."

For those in the Lower Seventy Percent, this was the subtext that spelled the end of the American Dream. America's rising productivity wasn't to be treated as a harvest in which all Americans were to share; the enrichment ideology of the nation's CEOs guaranteed a very different outcome. The fruits of our economy's rising productivity were to be redirected to those at the very top.

FDR's operating system for the American economy had been built on the ethically responsible premise that working Americans deserved to share in the economy's rising productivity and its rising prosperity. So what if the greed of the capitalist elites had to be held in check? President Roosevelt had little respect for the boundless greed of those he disparaged as "economic royalists."

Reagan's operating system canceled out FDR's more honorable approach. Those at the top were to be enriched beyond measure; those in the Lower 70% were to be left behind – further and further behind. The fruits of the economy's rising productivity weren't to be shared among all Americans, they were to be monopolized by the nation's economic elites.

Dozens of other measures, large and small, were added to the mix. Some of them came from Congress, in response to the entreaties of lobbyists, and some from the Supreme Court. Robert Reich's latest book, *Saving Capitalism: For the Many, Not the Few,* lays out many of the elements that became part of this shift; I won't try to repeat them here. Frank Levy and

Peter Temin also deepen the story in their study, "Inequality and Institutions in 20th Century America," published by the National Bureau of Economic Research.

Let's turn now to the hidden rationalizations by which those of great wealth justify their privileges. The central rationalizations of Enrichment Capitalism work more or less like this:

> *"Since I am wealthy, I am a person of very high status."*
>
> *"Since I am a person of very high status, I am also a person of great merit."*
>
> *"Since I am a person of great merit, I deserve to be exceptionally well compensated."*
>
> *"Since I am exceptionally well compensated, I have become quite wealthy."*
>
> *"And since I am quite wealthy, I am therefore a person of very high status."*
>
> *Wash. Rinse. Repeat.*

But it's not enough, is it, to rationalize the rewards captured by the barons at society's highest reaches. Society must also rationalize the scant paychecks received by its very weakest members. These rationalizations are the mirror image of those that ratify enrichment at the top:

> *"Since they are poor, they are people of very low status."*
>
> *"Since they are people of very low status, they are also people of very little merit."*
>
> *"Since they are people of very little merit, their wages should be quite low."*
>
> *"Since their wages are very low, they continue to be quite poor."*

*"And since they are quite poor, they continue
to be people of very low status."*

It's the Morality Play approach to labor economics, is it not? Think about it. Since they are wealthy, those at the top "deserve" what others might see as obscene levels of compensation.

And since those at the bottom are so poor and of such low status, their terrible social status proves that they "deserve" to be very badly paid.

It is a con game, of course, but one we've been taught to accept since we were small. Name a children's fairy tale that teaches kids to admire labor unions. Give up? Now name a fairy tale that teaches children to admire great wealth. More than we can count, right? And that's the point, isn't it? In the rationalized culture of Enrichment Capitalism, the wealthy are to be admired and the impoverished are to be perpetually underpaid.

Why does this sort of corruption take such deep root? Why does it survive and prosper?

We are in the presence of human failings so ancient that they regularly caught the attention of Old Testament prophets. Where there is prosperity, there is temptation. Temptation is eternal.

But what about corruption? Although temptation is eternal, corruption is a *choice.*

And in the Reagan era, America's elites made their choice. They embraced corruption. They switched off Prosperity Capitalism, despite its genuine virtues, and replaced it with the naked greed of Enrichment Capitalism.

And this leads us to an insight that our pundits do their best to hide. Capitalism is a powerful system, but its leaders will always be exposed to intense temptation. The leaders of wise nations recognize the lure of temptation but they do all they can to prevent it from degenerating into corruption.

The leaders of a foolish nation do the reverse. They embrace corruption. They permit systemic corruption to become a way of life.

Capitalism doesn't have to be corrupt. But if capitalism is to operate honorably, all of us have to be vigilant. Grass roots Americans have to be vigilant; elected officials have to be vigilant; and the operating system that guides our economy has to outlaw our descent into systemic corruption.

When those who called themselves "free market conservatives" took over, the people of our nation had grown weary. Our attention had wandered. And before anyone quite realized what was happening, the forces of systemic corruption had taken over. Free market conservatives hated Prosperity Capitalism. They desperately wanted the weak to be impoverished and the strong to become exceedingly rich.

What we call "Inequality" isn't an accident of history. It's the inevitable result of rules adopted to promote systemic corruption. We cannot outlaw Temptation, but we can outlaw Corruption. Capitalism is a wonderful system when its behavior is constrained by wise rules. Capitalism can become a dreadfully corrupt system when those who write its rules are working from within a worldview of rationalized corruption.

It is time to set aside all the false explanations that seek to distract us from the reality of our time. "Prosperity Capitalism" served our nation well – it gave us an honorable and patriotic way of running our capitalist economy. Enrichment Capitalism gives us a much more corrupt way of operating our economy. It is never safe to take away the rules that prevent the forces of systemic corruption from gaining the upper hand.

The fruits of America's rising productivity rightfully belong to all Americans, not just those at the top. America cannot be a healthy nation if the fruits of its rising productivity are to be forever withheld from three-quarters of the nation's workforce, if the benefits of the American Dream are to be limited only to the rich and the powerful.

Prosperity Capitalism is much the healthier and more patriotic choice. Yes, globalism is a challenge, and yes, it will be a challenge for a long time to come. But we cannot let the pressures of globalization become the alibi that permits the forces of systemic corruption to capture control of the American economy.

The American people made Prosperity Capitalism work before. We can make it work again.

The **Federal Government** *changed* sides.

Prosperity Capitalism was thrown aside.

Enrichment Capitalism took control.

★

Chapter Seven

Craftsmanship
ARE ECONOMISTS PART OF THE PROBLEM?

"They have yet to notice the difference between cost signals and wealth signals"

IF A DOCTOR MISTREATS A PATIENT, his license to practice medicine can be lifted. If a lawyer mistreats a client, the lawyer can be disbarred. But what about economists? If an economist tells the President that the nation's economy is doing fine, and then the nation's real estate market crashes, its largest banks collapse, massive federal bailouts are required, and millions are thrown out of work, what sort of discipline will the economist receive? Most likely none. And who will investigate the university that trained him? No one.

So economists, these theorists of market forces, draw their salaries from within a specialized labor market in which good rationalizations for amoral behavior are likely to bring even higher rewards than critical analyses of dangerous choices. So much for the notion that market competition will always be a source of rising quality!

Economists want their profession to have its cake and eat it too. They want their profession to be thought of as scientific and value-neutral; at the same time, as individual economists, they also want to be hired as legitimizers of the status quo. These flaws have been with us for a long time; as a result, those whom we call "Economists" regularly play key roles in the perpetuation of America's stuckness. It is a profession whose flaws are more extensive than we might realize; let's work through a few of them.

Temptation is Eternal, Corruption is a Choice

One might expect economists to champion the practice of cause-and-effect reasoning. One might expect them to warn us, therefore, about capitalism and its central risk.

Capitalism generates prosperity.

Prosperity stimulates temptation.

And, in an unrestrained society, temptation soon ripens into corruption. It begins as personal corruption and then ripens into systemic corruption.

The leaders of a wise society will use rules to prevent temptation from turning into corruption; in a foolish society, unwise leaders will give a green light to corruption – then they'll hold out their hands, seeking their cut!

Temptation is eternal; corruption is a choice.

If economics were an honorable profession, wouldn't its first message to its new students always be a warning about temptation, and the risk of temptation ripening into corruption? Wouldn't economists have a professional obligation to promote anti-corruption watchfulness?

Let's push this question a little further. History teaches us that global capitalism has always been brutal in its pursuit of wealth. Take Sven Beckert's book, *The Empire of Cotton,* an extraordinary history of global capitalism and its endless immorality. The wealth of England's nineteenth century cotton merchants rested indirectly on the slave economy of the American South. Southern planters had a global advantage. They had obtained their farmlands for almost nothing, given that federal troops were more than willing to get rid of the Native Americans who had long called them home. And southern planters also had a nearly free labor force; slaves had to be maintained but they didn't have to be paid. The soils of the South were suited to the cultivation of high grade cotton. Think of it. Free land. Cheap labor. A cotton-friendly climate. It all represented a large, stable, and inexpensive source of cotton for the cotton mills of Manchester and central England.

Think of it. A complete capitalist ecosystem, as it were, born of systemic corruption. We take Economics in college and we always hear about Adam Smith and the virtues of free trade. But who teaches us that capitalism, left to its own devices, will lead its followers down paths of systemic corruption and the creation of vast fortunes on the backs of slave labor? Well. It would be impolite to take note of capitalism's unsightly business practices, wouldn't it? Unprofessional, right?

We aren't taught to look for corruption because corruption requires regulation and a nation's economic professors presently function as the first line of defense against something as unseemly as the regulatory spirit.

An honest way of teaching capitalist economics would examine the full range of the corruptions that have been at its heart for much of its history.

On the eve of the American Civil War, cotton exports represented sixty-one percent of the USA's entire export trade. The firm known then as Brown Brothers made much of its early fortune by working as cotton brokers, profiting greatly from the financing and sale of southern cotton. This firm survives today as Brown Brothers Harriman. Corruption, abuse, and massive enrichment have been central themes in the practice of global capitalism for quite a long time; to imagine that such practices no longer exist is to close our eyes to the dark realities of terrible labor practices throughout much of the Third World.

Armed theft and capitalist enrichment have been a staple of human history for centuries. For a visit to one of the earliest and most brutal chapters in this long history of shameful conduct, pick up Charles Mann's *1493* and read his discussion of how Spain turned Peruvians into slaves and stole from Peru an entire mountain's worth of almost pure silver. Peru's fabulous silver mine at Potosi could have been a source of wealth for Peruvians; instead the people of Peru were enslaved at gunpoint and forced to work their own country's silver mines on Spain's behalf. Over many decades a vast fortune in silver was stolen, those riches fueling the rise of a Spanish merchant class.

But armed theft isn't the starting point of the neoliberal narrative. Neoliberal economists begin their story line with a hypothetical narrative in which expanding markets make it possible for honorable producers, honorable traders, and honorable customers to generate rising productivity, greater efficiency, and rising prosperity. It's a narrative that's embedded in the psyche of modern business. If "free markets" are "efficient," then surely they should be left to their own devices. Shouldn't they?

In the imaginary narratives of neoliberal economics, armed theft and other forms of systemic corruption are regularly airbrushed out of the picture. But omitting these brutal episodes from their fairy tale about "free market" capitalism doesn't change any of the realities that take place on the ground. The pursuit of excessive enrichment by the world's corporate and financial elites has always required systemic corruption.

There has always been a dark side to the cause-and-effect world in which those of great wealth have regularly bent the rest of the world to their aims. Neoliberal economists aren't in the business of helping us see these realities, and they're certainly not in the business of helping our society bring them under control.

What's Behind This?

Here's the story that we ought to tell ourselves. As Adam Smith properly observed, the clever use of technology in a single workshop makes that particular merchant more efficient. The clever use of technology in hundreds of workshops at the same time can make an entire nation more efficient, and under the right circumstances, these gains become a source of rising prosperity for the entire nation.

But these efficiencies arise only when the output of a nation's workshops can be sold as widely as possible. There's not enough demand in a single village to support the efficiencies of mass production and mass marketing. Producers have to have access to markets at quite some distance if they are to maximize their economies of scale.

With this observation in hand, the question that ought to come next is the question of who works for whom? Does a society's expanding economy exist to help the society as a whole prosper more fully? Or does a society's expanding economy exist to make its top capitalists incredibly rich, while leaving everyone else far behind?

Let's bring this home. Should the American economy exist to serve the larger interests of the entire nation? Or is the nation to see itself as subservient to its capitalist elites?

It's a rare capitalist, I fear, who will argue that the national interest takes precedence, that the selfish aims of the Top One Percent are to be subordinated to the best interests of the entire society. Hasn't it been true – throughout history – that the right of the elites to become excessively rich are thought to be more sacred than the well-being of the nations that host their operations?

And, therefore, hasn't it also been true that government normally steps into the role of enabler? With the nation's top politicians helping their nation's elites fulfill their most lavish ambitions? If this support requires the suppression of criticism and protest from below, then so be it.

President Franklin Roosevelt detested this worldview. He denounced the rise of those he called "Economic Royalists," and insisted in the midst of Depression and war on passing laws to curb the practice of unlimited self-enrichment. As a counterweight to these abuses, he did what he could to promote the rise of organized labor.

To leaders like Franklin Delano Roosevelt, there is always an alternative answer. The central mission of the American economy is to help the American people thrive. It makes sense to modulate the greed of the nation's capitalist elite so that the greater prosperity of the entire nation can be protected.

That, at least, was FDR's answer. Yes, as the Bible reminds us, temptation is eternal. But corruption is a choice. Under FDR's Rules, the needs of the whole nation took precedence over the personal ambitions of America's leading capitalists.

That has not been the central message of neoliberal economics. Neoliberal economists tacitly play the role of discrediting FDR's argument. Too many neoliberal economists function as rationalizers for limitless enrichment at the top.

There's no point in skirting the issue. Not everyone in the neoliberal world operates by its playbook, but the playbook is well-known. Rationalize enrichment for the top; rationalize stagnation for everyone else.

The purpose of neoliberal economics is to tell the Adam Smith story but discourage young people from raising FDR's objections. Unregulated capitalism, the neoliberals will say, is best. "Market forces" are smarter than government, so government should leave them alone.

It's a scam. Neoliberal economists are trained to rationalize the enrichment goals of an irresponsible elite. They aren't trained to warn the nation away from the systemic corruption that invariably accompanies excessive enrichment at the top.

An Economics profession with an honorable sense of mission would bring genuine ethical clarity to its role. It would know that America's well-being comes first. It would know that America cannot be a healthy nation without a civic spirit of three-sixty responsibility. It would want all of this nation's many parts to operate honorably and well. An honorable *economy.* Honorable *technologies,* that respect Nature's well-being. Honorable *communities,* with the era of ghettoes receding in the rearview mirror. Honorable *elections* and honorable *politics*, with high barriers to the practice of systemic corruption.

An honorably-conceived Economics would always be on the alert against the forces of systemic corruption. It would warn us, again and again, never to forget that ancient truth: "Temptation is eternal. Corruption is a choice. A wise nation does all it can to prevent systemic corruption from taking root."

In the eyes of today's neoliberals, though, corruption isn't just a choice; it's the preferred choice.

Now let's dig into some of the details.

The GDP Economy and the Wealth Economy

One of the major weaknesses of contemporary Economics as a field of study is that its practitioners are taught to focus much more on the economy's output side than on its asset side.

Contemporary economists, therefore, are more facile in discussing GDP issues than they are in spotting difficulties on the balance sheet side of the economy, such as asset bubbles and unrealistic notions about stock market returns.

In other words, they aren't properly equipped to help the nation wrestle responsibly with questions of wealth and enrichment.

And with their biases, economists are ill-suited for stepping up to some of their most significant responsibilities. They can't see corruption coming. They can't see bubbles coming until it's too late. They aren't ready to guide the nation away from its false choices and toward its higher responsibilities.

Take, for example, the simple question of whether financial markets are "smart," as Alan Greenspan liked to say, and able to take care of themselves without government regulation.

We already know how that turned out. Too much real estate lending, too much securitization of poor quality mortgages, and a very narrow escape in 2008 from a complete financial meltdown. As Tim Geithner later observed, America's banks at the depth of the crisis were within three days of turning off the nation's ATMs.

What is it that economists are not trained to see?

For starters, they aren't trained to recognize the distinction between product markets and asset markets. What ought to be an elementary point never shows up as part of their worldview.

In a product market, a rising price sends a *rising cost signal*. If prices rise for Florida oranges, say, buyers are likely to respond by cutting back on their purchases. In a product market, rising prices will generate dampening feedback, and because they do, product markets tend to be self-stabilizing. Self-stabilizing markets don't have a great need for government regulation. Economists seem to have this figured out.

But curiously they seem not have noticed how this logic changes when one switches from product markets to asset markets.

In an asset market (corporate equities, real estate), a rising price also sends a *rising wealth signal*. "If I owned more of this asset, I'd be getting *wealthier* right now." While rising cost signals in a product market can discourage buying, the rising wealth signals that occur in asset markets can stimulate even *more* buying.

Sometimes this process becomes so powerful that asset markets destabilize themselves. Rising asset values intensify their wealth signals. Bubbles take hold. Prices rise, and rise some more. No one wants to take away the punch bowl. And then the market crashes. Asset prices plunge, and as owners see their wealth shrinking, they unload their holdings even faster. The crash gets worse. Firms that thought they were solvent realize that they're about to go broke.

Product markets have a built-in tendency to stabilize themselves. Economists know this. But it seems to escape them that asset markets aren't necessarily self-stabilizing.

Because the risks of instability are significantly greater in asset markets than they are in product markets, a nation's asset markets inherently require greater supervision than its product markets. It was a terrible mistake for Greenspan and others to have missed the contrasting effects of rising prices. Assumptions of stability that worked well in product markets were not to be trusted in the world of asset markets.

It is a striking thing to see even the biggest names in economics miss a point that ought to be so elementary. Yale's Robert Shiller, author of *Irrational Exuberance*, understands the operation of crowd psychology in the stock market as well as anyone, but even Shiller fails to put his finger on the elemental distinction between price increases that send cost signals and price increases that send wealth signals.

But this is just the sort of weakness that's to be expected of a profession whose theories are focused more heavily on the GDP side of the economy than on its balance sheet side.

This weakness also shows up in the tendency of economists to misunderstand the issue of long-run stock market returns.

It was imagined by many economists, in the long stock market boom of the 1980s and 1990s, that stock market returns would always average seven or eight or nine percent a year. Pension fund portfolio managers were led astray by these promises on any number of occasions, to the long-run detriment of the funds they were managing.

It should have been a matter of common sense, even for those raised within the blinkered theories of neoliberal economics, to have doubted that total stock market capitalization would rise faster than GDP growth over the long run.

If the GDP grows at three percent a year, wouldn't it stand to reason that the total value of U.S. equities would also grow at three percent a year? Yes, individuals who regularly reinvest all their dividends can grow their own portfolios more rapidly, but that's not the heart of the story.

The underlying reality is that growth in the asset side of the economy has always been tied to growth in its output side. Long run growth in the size of the output economy (GDP) is the pacing variable that sets the long-term growth rate for the nation's equity markets.

Let's imagine the sort of exercise that we'd be put through as students, if we were being trained in school to understand these connections.

We'd be given two very straightforward data sets. For total stock market capitalization, we'd use the Federal Reserve's Z-1 report, Table L-213, which tracks the value of stock market equities.

For total GDP, we'd rely on White House and Commerce Department data, although for the very earliest period in the graphs below, one would have to rely on other sources and make educated guesses.

Let's begin by calculating an obvious ratio – Stock Market Capitalization as a percent of Gross Domestic Product.

As you look at Figure 7.1, imagine yourself in the mid-1980s with a youthful interest in the stock market. Your experience is limited. You're just getting your feet wet. But you're about to go on an extraordinary ride. From the early 1980s to the spring of 2000, as you will see in the graph below, the Market Capitalization to GDP Ratio *quadruples!*

Anyone living through such a period might easily fall for the notion that stock market investing has become the path to ever-increasing personal wealth. "You'll have seven percent compound growth, ten percent, fifteen percent." In the go-go years of the 1990s, no claim seemed unreasonably high. People thought they understood the cause-and-effect forces at work. How wrong they were!

While Figure 7.1 suggests a story of extreme variation, the very next graph, Figure 7.2, provides an essential corrective.

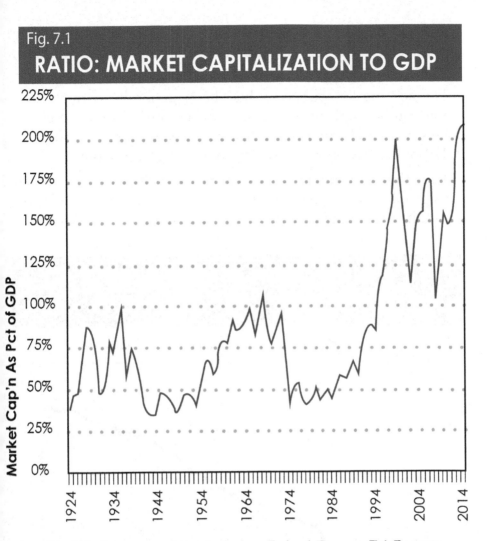

Fig. 7.1 Sources explained above. Federal Reserve Z-1 Reports, Table L-213. Commerce Department GDP data.

Figure 7.2, below, uses a semi-log scale in order to show us the long view.

Note each step on the left-hand scale is therefore ten times larger than the previous step. $0.01 trillion. $0.1 trillion. $1 trillion. $10 trillion. $100 trillion. In other words, $10 billion, $100 billion, $1 trillion, and so on.

GDP growth over time is represented by the continuously dotted line; the second line, the one that jumps around, represents market capitalization values over time.

If stock market publicists had been generally correct, how should this graph have changed over time? Growth rates for Market Capitalization would have exceeded growth rates for GDP, not just in short bursts, but as an ongoing pattern.

Had this been the way the real world behaved, the lines in this graph would have diverged. Growth in total stock market capitalization would have far outpaced the growth in GDP.

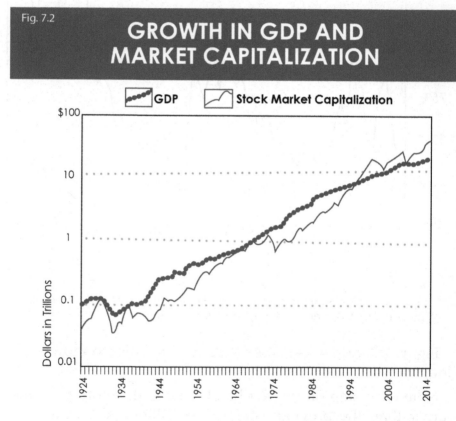

Fig. **7.2** Same sources as Fig. 7.1 GDP numbers from Department of Commerce and Economic Reports of the President. Market Capitalization figures from Federal Reserve's Z-1 reports, Table L-213.

Is that what we see? Not hardly. Market Capitalization totals fluctuate, but always in the general vicinity of GDP. The hyper-growth optimists – as the graph teaches us – were quite simply wrong. Stock market capitalization has been tethered to GDP for decades and decades. Sometimes market values rise a little faster than GDP, and sometimes they experience temporary slumps. There has been a modest uptick over the past two decades, mostly caused by the switch from Prosperity Capitalism to Enrichment Capitalism, but we had best think of this as a one-time correction.

The core reality is hard to avoid. Over the long run, the stock market grows in tandem with GDP. It doesn't outrace GDP.

In other words, the bubble years of the Reagan-Bush-Clinton era were a poor guide to the long run realities of our economy. Total market capitalization may grow at rates that far exceed GDP for short periods, but over the long run, total market capitalization and Gross Domestic Product will experience very similar growth rates.

That's one key point – a point of great interest to pension fund managers all across the U.S.

There is a second key point to be considered, quite different from the first.

It's true that the stock market doesn't grow at eight percent a year. And it's true that even with reinvested dividends, it's not easy for an individual investor to sustain real portfolio growth of eight percent or more.

But the notion that asset wealth *can* grow at eight percent a year has nevertheless taken hold among the nation's elites. And what's more, it's no longer just an interesting hypothesis; it has been turned into an entitlement ideology, especially by those at the very top end of the Top One Percent. If wealth can grow at eight percent a year, or so they imagine, then it has become perfectly natural for them to believe that compensation at the very top *ought to grow* at eight percent a year.

What started out as a *growth hypothesis* (even though it was false) was almost immediately repackaged as an *enrichment entitlement*.

Beginning in the Reagan years, those at the top end of the Top One Percent set out to grow their personal compensation at eight percent a year. It was an entitlement, dammit, and folks better get out of their way. They were determined to cash in, no matter what sort of damage their behaviors might generate.

There was a small detail, of course, a tiny little obstacle. If those at the top are to grow their personal incomes at eight percent a year, in an economy that grows by three percent a year, those at the bottom will have to accept . . . what? Almost no growth at all, right?

And so – at its heart – that's where America's "Inequality" problem really comes from. *The poor have to stay poor so that personal compensation for the super-rich can shoot forward at seven or eight percent a year.*

Fig. 7.3
AVERAGE INCOME PER TAX UNIT* IN 2014 DOLLARS

Income Group	1945	1981	2007	2014
Bottom 90%	$18,700	$33,200	$35,900	$32,400
Next 5%	$48,700	$104,400	$140,600	$138,500
Next 4%	$74,000	$143,700	$230,700	$231,300
Next 0.5%	$160,200	$231,200	$477,100	$459,900
Next 0.4%	$284,500	$355,100	$914,800	$852,400
Next 0.09%	$687,500	$774,500	$3,060,400	$2,680,100
Top 0.01%	$2,113,100	$2,913,600	$20,984,600	$17,179,300

*Capital Gains Excluded

Figure 7.3 Saez op cit. Author's calculations.

This brings us to the heart of the story, the story that neoliberal economists won't explain because they've been conditioned not to look.

Let's reach back to the Saez database I used earlier, and take another look at the numbers.

All the numbers in this table have been restated in 2014 dollars.

Let's focus on two rows, the rows in bold. What I want to compare are the income growth rates for the working people in the Bottom 90% with the average growth rates for working people in the Top 1% of the Top One Percent.

Let's start with the era of Prosperity Capitalism, the years from 1945 through 1981.

For those in the Bottom 90%, incomes (in 2014 dollars) rose from $18,700 to $33,200.

For those in the Bottom 90%, average incomes were up by 78% in 1981 compared with 1945.

For those in the Top 0.01%, average incomes were up by 38%.

Incomes had grown more rapidly for Americans in the Bottom 90% than for Americans in the Top 0.01%.

Now shift to the era of Enrichment Capitalism, and look first at what happens between 1981 and 2007 – from the beginning of Reagan's presidency to the eve of the Crash that occurred in 2008.

For those in the Bottom 90%, real pretax earnings barely rise at all. $33,200 in 1981; $35,900 in 2007, an increase of only 8 percent.

For those in the Top 0.01%, real pretax earnings explode. $2.9 million in 1981, almost $21 million in 2007, an increase of seven hundred twenty percent!

Now, perhaps, it's clear why I propose that we refer to the first period, 1945 to 1981, as the era of Prosperity Capitalism. It was a time in which pretax earnings rose faster for those at the bottom than for those at the top.

And perhaps it's also clear why I argue that the more recent period, from 1981 onward, should be thought of as an era of Enrichment Capitalism. For those at the bottom, earnings during this more recent period more or less stalled out.

But for those at the very very top, earnings were *seven hundred twenty percent higher in 2007* than they had been in 1981, a mere 26 years earlier.

Enrichment Capitalism teaches those at the top to flatter themselves beyond measure, to see themselves as entitled to unbelievably high rates of compensation growth.

FDR's Rules had kept the lid on this kind of corruption. Reagan's Rules removed the lid and invited those at the very top to enrich themselves as fast as they could, even if their enrichment were to come at everyone else's expense.

This isn't really about market forces, is it? It's not about the "market value" of CEOs. No. These are returns to power. These are returns to greed and abusiveness. These are returns to collusion and to systemic corruption. They are so lucrative that inevitably they reinforce the malign behaviors that make them possible in the first place. Greed, abuse, collusion, and systemic corruption – in an era of Enrichment Capitalism, every major sin is to be rewarded and reinforced.

Temptation is eternal. Corruption is a choice.

Under Reagan's Rules, those at the very top of the American economy have decreed that systemic corruption is not only their choice, it is their due.

This is the modern capitalism's ugly side, the side that neoliberal economists have been trained to rationalize or even ignore.

Their training keeps them focused elsewhere. They are not properly trained to help the nation's elected officials champion Prosperity Capitalism. They are not trained to defend the interests of the Bottom 90%, or the Bottom 70%, as the case may be.

But they are trained to take on the lucrative task of rationalizing systemic corruption. So even when they "see" corruption, they don't really see it. It's not real to them because their profession has taught them that "markets are smart" – a falsehood. Their profession hasn't taught them to realize that the long arc of capitalism always bends toward systemic corruption.

Yes, neoliberal economists have a serious blind spot. And beyond that, they have a blind spot about their blind spot. They don't know what it is they don't know. One of my Stanford economics profs confessed in class one day that he'd earned his Ph.D. without ever learning to read a Balance Sheet.

A Profession in Need of Reform

When economists blow a major call, as they sometimes do, where's the penalty? Economics as a profession appreciates analytic cleverness on small issues, but is so wary of applying moral reasoning to the nation's larger issues that even an economist as eminent as Joseph Stiglitz will write a lengthy policy analysis for the Roosevelt Institute without once using the word "corruption." What an odd thing it is to see a Nobel Prize winner so conditioned by the norms of his peculiar profession that he cannot bring himself to apply the words "systemic corruption" to the forces currently driving the American economy.

It's time for the "discipline" of Economics to be publicly called out for its role in disguising the presence of systemic corruption, both in our national economy and in the global economy.

It is also time for Economics as a discipline to toss out its founding charter and start over.

Corruption is an ever-present temptation in any capitalist economy. We cannot prevent its rise with an Economics profession that takes its cues from Harry Potter. "He Who Must Not Be Named" is Harry Potter's foe. Systemic Corruption in our economy is America's foe, but if it's "The Problem That Must Not Be Named," how is anyone else to find out? If it is to be properly controlled, its presence must first be properly acknowledged.

When systemic corruption takes hold of an economy as powerful as ours, millions of lower income Americans are sure to be victimized. When abuses at the top become as acute as they are today, economists ought to be the ones who swing into action as America's First Responders.

When major industries build their fortunes on technologies that imperil the well-being of the global climate, economists ought to be among our nation's First Responders.

When America's cities find themselves being ghettoized by corrupted market forces, economists ought to be among our nation's First Responders.

Economists should never accept as their mission the task of rationalizing systemic corruption.

Economics should be a discipline that engages itself in setting rigorous responsibility standards for each of the economy's major cause-and-effect systems.

The American people are going to want the benefits of a growing economy to be appropriately shared with the entire workforce.

A wise public will want to see their nation living by a spirit of Three-Sixty Responsibility. They will want to see the American economy protecting Nature, not abusing Nature. And they will want America's economists to help them move America in that direction.

A wise public will want to see a healthy economy doing its part to create cities and towns in which all neighborhoods prosper.

A wise public wants to see its corporate leaders respecting the nation's elected officials, not sneaking in through the back door in hopes of corrupting them at every turn.

Economists of late have spent too much time being part of the problem and too little time being part of the solution. It's time for decades of faulty conditioning to be shaken off. It's time for economists to accept the kind of First Responder role they ought to have been playing from the very beginning.

Capitalism can be a system that generates all sorts of positive benefits. It can be a system of which we would be rightfully proud. But first our nation needs to strip its leaders of the notion that capitalism can't be capitalism unless it's permitted to wallow in systemic corruption. And our economists should be at our sides, helping the nation secure an end to capitalist corruption.

Economists live within an unspoken pact.

Never acknowledge the presence of *systemic* corruption.

It's sad.

When systemic corruption starts to sneak in, economists ought to be **America's First Responders**

Getting America **UnStuck**
The Politics of **Character** & **Craftsmanship**

americaunstuck.com

Chapter Eight

Craftsmanship

THE URBAN POVERTY CHALLENGE

"Can we free our cities from Jim Crow Lite?"

WHAT SHALL WE MAKE OF AMERICA'S urban future, America's future as a middle class nation, and America's future as a racially diverse nation?

This is surely one of our country's most complex domestic challenges. One winces to see even our most capable politicians dancing away from the need, while many others stoke racial fears whenever they see opportunities for gain.

The Civil Rights Movement solved an important problem. Were black Americans to be treated as equals by the public schools? At restaurants, at motels? When buying homes, when seeking jobs, when registering to vote? With *Brown vs. Board of Education,* with the Civil Rights Act of 1964, with the Voting Rights Act of 1965, white America replied with an equivocal, "Yes, sort of."

Through these legal changes, and the social changes they also called forth, we Americans achieved a higher level of multi-racial tolerance than we had known before. But these gains have had a flip side. Black Americans with middle class skills and status were afforded the chance to operate on more of an equal footing with their white middle class peers. And black Americans at all levels have had better chances to run candidates, vote in elections, and place many of their candidates in public office.

But deeper rifts remain. The racial imprint of a long-standing "Two Americas" Culture is painfully visible in the social geographies of American cities. One America lives in middle class neighborhoods; the other America lives in conditions of pervasive poverty. We middle class whites are less likely to be racist toward middle class blacks but just as likely as ever to act on racist fears of underclass blacks, Hispanics, and others who for decades have been pushed into ghettoes by the fears and the intolerance of the privileged.

In other words, within the middle class, we have softened our Two Americas Culture, but across the boundaries of prosperity and poverty, our Two Americas Culture seems to have hardened. If the clean sheets hanging on the line belong to someone poor, much of today's white middle class might willingly fling ashes against them. So much for middle class "character." Our character takes a clobbering from our passions.

This isn't new. It is a separation that has been with us for a good long time.

Someday, we tell ourselves, we really ought to overcome. Someday.

Someday . . . but not today. Or any time soon.

How are we to think about this? Or better, how are we to rethink where we are, and how are we to imagine where we might be? As we do, will we find ourselves once again chipping away at major problems with modestly incremental adjustments? Rather than hungering for a transformational journey that could help us be, well, free at last?

In tomorrow's urban America, will we accept the same sort of systemic corruption that has been the hallmark of yesterday's urban America? Or will we bring it to a halt?

The diagnostic journey has been available for some time. *American Apartheid: Segregation and the Making of the Underclass,*

by Douglas S. Massey and Nancy A. Denton, describes our nation's journey of ghettoization in some detail. If it's diagnostic insight we want, *American Apartheid* is a good place to start. Many other books have fleshed its central story even further.

But what about our prescriptive vision? That's the question that scares us; it's *so hard*.

How are we to *change?*

Well, first of all there has to be a "we." And then there has to be a game plan. Here I will sketch the thought process ahead.

There are five larger gains we have to aim for – first – in order to set the stage.

First, we shall have to call an end to Elite Enrichment Capitalism. We have to commit our nation to the restoration of Prosperity Capitalism. Enrichment Capitalism damages the nation as a whole; it will never be America's healthy choice. Ever. It's the wrong system for our nation as a whole, and for those who live in chronic poverty, its effects are especially harsh. The proper way to kickstart an urban progress agenda is with a responsible capitalism agenda.

Second, we have to call forth large numbers of caring and forceful people who are ready to be part of the solution. They're waiting for the right leadership, they're waiting for the work ahead to be properly organized, and they're waiting for the emergence of a coalition strong enough to get America over the hump. Show them the far-sighted coalition they've been longing for, and they'll step forward, ready to do their part.

Third, we have to commit ourselves to the conviction that the culture of poverty can be overcome by those who are presently trapped within it. Yes, there are all kinds of obstacles. But almost all of us have a better side, and will respond constructively once a climate of mutual trust has been established.

Fourth, we have to commit ourselves to a long time horizon. Racist patterns of real estate development have been with us for many long decades. White prosperity over here, black poverty over there. Anglo prosperity over here, Hispanic poverty over there. Neighborhood by neighborhood, these separatist patterns need to be slowly and gently dissolved. It's a journey that will take many years – at least a generation and perhaps two or three. Its markers, its forward steps, have to become so ingrained that ongoing progress eventually settles in as a routine part of who we are.

And, fifth, we need grace. It's so easy in today's America to get our hearts all locked up. But we are not without help. There are saints among us, if you will, friends who already possess the deeper serenity that such an adventure requires. And almost all of us in fits and starts have experienced our own capacity for warmth. Prayer helps. Faith helps. However the Lord speaks to us, let us open our hearts and listen. The journey toward tomorrow's healthy cities is a journey that begins with love.

What has to change for America's cities to become healthy places to live for everyone?

For starters, our prescriptive image of the journey ahead has to change. Up till now, we have thought of urban poverty as something one responds to with small, incremental steps. Modest adjustments here, modest adjustments there, a few more resources here, a few more resources there.

What lies ahead will take a higher level of craftsmanship than this. If the journey ahead is to take us to a successful future, we will need the same sort of spirit Cummins was able to generate. Awaken a transformational vision, and then through persistence and dedication, ripen that vision into a living reality.

This is not just a journey of helping high potential individuals escape from the tough neighborhoods where they were raised; this is a journey that takes place within neighborhoods as all their residents weave together actions of mutual support, feelings of trust, and stronger aspirations for everyone.

And it's not a journey that takes place only within poverty neighborhoods. It is a journey of transformation for prosperous neighborhoods as well.

It is a journey toward different and better schools, schools that reach every child.

We saw a hint of that dream in an earlier chapter.

It is also a journey toward labor markets that won't leave America's teens out in the cold. The labor market has to be more welcoming, more vigorous, and always full of promise.

It is a journey toward a culture of two-parent families. "Learn. Earn. Marry. Have kids. Raise them together." It's not society's only norm, but for a great many of us, it is still our best choice. And the best choice for our children.

It is a journey toward a culture of middle class ambition. Save money toward a home. Save money toward college. Save money toward retirement.

It is a journey toward self-restraint and a culture of settling disagreements calmly and peacefully.

It is a journey toward a more reconciling style of policing.

It is a journey toward safe ways of getting high and avoidance of more dangerous ways of getting high.

It is a journey toward treating addiction as a medical problem and away from treating it as a law enforcement problem.

It's a journey away from black market drugs and toward regulated drugs, away from the reach of gangs, toward a safer system of regulated drug sales that shrivels up the markets served by urban gangs.

It is a journey away from using prisons to warehouse the mentally ill, a journey toward reviving the nation's ability to provide sensible mental health services to all who need them.

It is a journey toward the acceptance of affordable housing in small doses in all neighborhoods, in every city, so that ghettoized housing patterns can slowly fade away.

It is a journey toward the conversion of rental units in low-income neighborhoods into tiny homes or condos that residents can buy and own.

It is a journey toward creeping gentrification of what were once high poverty neighborhoods. It is a journey toward affordable housing in every neighborhood. Who's to tell us that affordable housing can't be posh enough to play a role in all neighborhoods? As America ages, affordable housing choices in all neighborhoods will ripen into something that's essential everywhere.

It is a journey in which all of us learn that everything works better when all of us become "givers of safety." This will be a hard lesson for many, given our conditioning. Safety – so our urban cultures say – is something that has to be taken, by force, from an angry environment. Those views have hardened into a misguided habit. In the higher vision of tomorrow's cities, safety becomes real when we learn to define ourselves not as "takers of safety" but as "givers of safety."

It is a journey in which all of us learn that everything works better when all of us share a widened sense of loyalty. The more loyal we become toward the wider circles of our communities, the more vibrant our communities will become.

In other words, it is a journey in which the faulty behaviors of a thousand prejudiced yesterdays are slowly laid aside, in favor of the redemptive behaviors of a thousand wiser tomorrows.

So many journeys, each with its own transformational content. And all of those journeys, unfolding together, blending into a larger transformation of towns and cities across America.

Late in the film *North by Northwest*, Cary Grant clings to a ledge on the face of Mount Rushmore, with Eva Marie Saint dangling below and Martin Landau grinding his shoe maliciously on

Cary Grant's fingers, hoping to break his grip.

That's pretty much what middle class America has long done to the nation's poor. Stepped on their fingers in hopes they'd lose their grip and plunge into the permanent underclass. "No, jobs are scarce and you can't have *my* job." "No, good schools are scarce and you can't send your kids to *my* school." "No, decent housing is scarce and we won't permit you to live in *our* neighborhood." "No, drug use is a *criminal* problem, and you won't be given any medical help for it." And on and on.

Alfred Hitchcock's movie spares Cary Grant and Eva Marie Saint, but middle class and upper class Americans haven't been nearly so generous toward the nation's poor.

The journey toward healthy cities begins with middle class America removing its shoe from the fingers of all those clinging to ledges somewhere.

But it's more, much more. It has to be a journey away from poor choices, all up and down the line, for everyone. Faulty choices by middle class Americans. Faulty choices by the Top One Percent. Faulty choices by the nation's poor.

It has to be an all-sided journey of mutual redemption. Redemption for middle class Americans, who willingly back away from damaging institutional practices. Redemption for poor Americans, who willingly commit to wiser choices about their lives. And redemption for America's elites, through the creation of job opportunities for everyone.

Ghettoes are what we do to ourselves when we don't mind being snobs and making other people suffer. It's not precisely a matter of incinerator ashes on someone else's clean sheets; it's the same sort of irresponsibility, yes, but far more intense.

America's heritage of Systemic Corruption has taught all too many of us to give a knowing wink to those who step on other people's fingers in order to make them lose their grip.

The Politics of Character and Craftsmanship isn't about knocking the poor and the weak off whatever ledges they now cling to. It's about the exact opposite. First we cut a bargain in which we all agree to act like good neighbors. And then, in acting like good neighbors, in time we discover what a pleasure it is to *become* good neighbors.

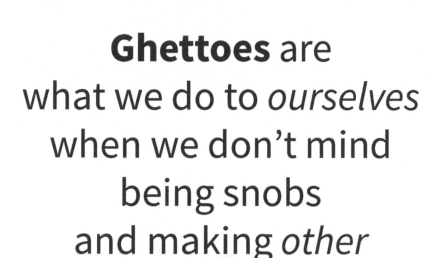

Ghettoes are
what we do to *ourselves*
when we don't mind
being snobs
and making *other*
people suffer.

Getting America **UnStuck**
The Politics of **Character** & **Craftsmanship**

americaunstuck.com

★

Chapter Nine

Craftsmanship
THE RETIREMENT CHALLENGE

"Large-scale problem, small-scale answers."

AS WE HAVE SEEN FROM THE POPULATION CHART displayed in the first chapter, America is in the early stages of a vast demographic explosion. Those sixty-five and older will have doubled their numbers, and then some, by 2045. But the working age population? Very modest growth.

How is Social Security to survive? It's one of the cause-and-effect questions that we all want to duck. It makes our heads hurt to think about it. Social Security depends on tax receipts from working Americans and their employers to fund the benefits it pays to retirees, a formula that once worked well when there tens of millions of workers and not so many retirees, but one which is now fraying badly just as the nation's senior population begins to explode. It will take major changes to put Social Security on sound footing given our demographic upheaval.

One might think that a shift of this magnitude would capture the nation's attention and stir us to action. But the Politics of Systemic Corruption are meant to punish those who care and reward those who don't care. We end up ignoring such problems till it's very late in the game. Republicans have trapped themselves in their Morality Play rituals; cause-and-effect reasoning is off limits. Democrats and their advocacy groups fall well short of providing the foresight America requires.

And this lack of craftsmanship on the pension front has been the nation's way for quite some time. In the mid-1970s, I found myself in the midst of the pension issue as a union officer for the taxi drivers at Denver Yellow Cab. We called ourselves IDA, the Independent Drivers Association, a name our group had chosen in its break from the Teamsters several years earlier.[1]

The pension issue was taken up within IDA by a group of high seniority drivers who thought it was time for us to set up a modest pension program. It wouldn't be much, but it would do a little something for our highest seniority drivers once they retired. If memory serves, the program was meant to support drivers who had accumulated at least twenty years in the cab business. It was to be funded with an increase in union dues. Instead of paying dues of $8 a month, drivers would pay dues of $1 a shift. Once approved, the dues change was expected to generate a few thousand dollars a month for the IDA pension program.

As with any issue put up for a membership vote, there was controversy, but younger drivers were sympathetic enough with those who'd been driving for years that the proposal passed.

Perhaps three or four years later, a couple of government auditors stopped by our union hall. I was then IDA's president and still recall the warning they gave us. Our pension program wasn't "funded," they said – using a term I was not then familiar with.

Should the union ever go belly-up, its pool of capital would be too small to cover its lifetime obligations to its retirees. A

---

1 - To rally support in their battle to kick out the Teamsters, IDA's founders set up an after-hours joint as a hangout for their supporters. In other words, IDA was in the bar business even before it was officially in the union business. When IDA triumphed over the Teamsters, its founders rented a vacant machine shop just large enough to house not only a union office but also a bar. It was never entirely clear whether we were a union that happened to be in the bar business, or a bar that also happened to be in the union business.

pension program meets the "funded" test only by having enough money on hand to meet all its obligations even if its sponsoring body were to be dissolved. The auditors advised us to boost the union contribution by several thousand dollars a month and keep at it till our modest pension program was "fully funded."

We could not have boosted union contributions to the pension fund without raising our union dues, again, and this would have required membership approval in another vote. Was it likely that young drivers would have voted to raise their own dues another notch in order to please a pair of government auditors?

Only a fraction of the membership was likely to stay in the cab business long enough to benefit. To ask the question is to answer it. A vote to raise our dues even more – just to please the government – would have gone down in flames. We never even tried. For better or worse, IDA's modest pension was to remain unfunded. (And, yes, eventually the union did go belly-up.)

As with cab drivers, so too for much of the nation. Our diagnostic and prescriptive weaknesses, within IDA, were also the nation's weaknesses.

Any number of companies had launched pensions, back in those days, without first asking the "funded program" question. As cab drivers, we hadn't known how expensive it would be to create a funded pension program, and we were hardly alone. Folks at thousands of other companies hadn't realized it either.

But more to the point, we hadn't wanted to ask ourselves the "universal coverage" question. Wasn't there something morally wrong with creating a pension program devoted solely to those few among us who would eventually become career drivers? Wouldn't it have been smarter to have sought retirement accounts for everyone who drove a taxi at Yellow Cab, even if only for a few months?

Well, yes. A program that helped all drivers save toward retirement would have been fairer and more far-sighted.

As with eight hundred cab drivers in Denver, though, so too for the nation. Companies all across America had focused their pension promises on their high seniority employees, effectively diverting wages from short-term employees for the benefit of career employees.

But back to the question of defined benefit pensions and the funding hurdles that came with them. Anyone offering a defined benefit pension to a group of employees had to have solid answers to five tough questions. How many employees would end up being eligible? Would the sponsoring organization be as large and successful in the future as it appeared to be now? How much cash could the sponsor afford to set aside, each year, to fund the program? How much would these funds earn when responsibly invested? And how much could the sponsor reasonably promise to future retirees?

Five tough questions, five chances to make significant mistakes.

Underestimate the total size of tomorrow's retiree pool and one's program could be caught short.

Underestimate the risk that your organization might shrink with time and its capacity to sustain tomorrow's flow of contributions might shrink more drastically than anyone would have imagined.

Even with stable employment levels, guessing too low on how much was to be set aside every year would bring tomorrow's pension fund up short.

Overestimate potential earnings from the stock market and one's pension reserves could end up being much smaller than you expected.

Promise too much to future retirees and in time you'd find your program badly overextended.

With so many possibilities for ending up badly, those officials charged with writing rules for the nation's Defined Benefit pension programs felt an urgent obligation. Tighten the controls enough to ensure pension solvency even in the worst of times. If a company was to promise a stable pension to its future retirees, it had an obligation to get its numbers right. As federal standards were tightened, companies were forced to write larger and larger checks to their pension programs.

And it wasn't long till employers by the thousands found themselves backing away from "Defined Benefit" pension programs and replacing them with "Defined Contribution" savings programs.

This was a major jolt for millions. A Defined Contribution approach can work well for those who set up savings accounts in their twenties and contribute faithfully throughout their working lives. Its value isn't nearly as great to those who wait till their late thirties or early forties to start saving.

The story was different in the public sector. In most states, a Defined Benefit pension agreement between a local government and its employees is legally binding. The commitment, once made, has to be kept.

On this front, there's been good news and there's been bad news. Readers will be relieved to know that successful public employee pension programs outnumber unsuccessful programs.[2] On the other hand, faulty programs are still much too common.

Pension programs run by public agencies face exactly the same hurdles as those the private sector had created. (1)

---

2 - Pension Funding Task Force 2013, co-sponsored by the National Governors Association, the National Conference of State Legislatures, and nine other organizations. The largest public pension plans hold roughly $3.6 trillion in assets; of these, $2.7 trillion is held by properly funded plans and another $0.9 trillion by inadequately funded plans.

Agencies have to guess right about their own long-run future. Not every agency will be as large in twenty years as it is today. (2) Agencies have to guess right about the number of retirees that they'll one day be supporting. (3) Their promised benefits have to be affordable; extravagant promises will empty the till. (4) Fund Trustees have to be cautious in estimating stock market returns; it isn't safe to treat the stock market as a magic lamp capable of generating unlimited wealth. (5) Contributions to the pension fund from its government sponsor have to be large enough, year after year, to keep the program healthy.

It takes considerable wisdom to design a fund strong enough to meet all these tests at the same time, and yet that's the key to delivering on the promises being made to the agency's future retirees.

With wobbly standards of craftsmanship as a frequent norm, poor choices have been all too common. Public sector unions sometimes insist on pension benefits far too lavish for the agency they bargain with. Pension managers sometimes pretend the stock market will give them far higher returns than are likely. And local governments, especially in times of fiscal difficulty, have contributed less to their pension funds than was prudent.

Sometimes a local authority falls short on one count; sometimes a local authority falls short on several at the same time. Pension programs for the City of Detroit and the State of California have come to symbolize the harm that comes when public officials and pension trustees are too stressed to fulfill their long-term responsibilities.

The deeper lesson from the last half-century is that America requires a civic ethos of Character and Craftsmanship. These virtues have not been our long suit. Without the restraints of a wise civic ethos, one sees too many instances of snap decisions and bad outcomes. Our civic culture doesn't teach us to give rigorous thinking the respect it deserves.

But we shouldn't leave it there. Tomorrow's retirees have also been undercut by the rise of Enrichment Capitalism and the abandonment of Prosperity Capitalism. In an America of steadily rising incomes, the pension challenges I have been discussing wouldn't have been quite as troubling.

But that hasn't been the America we live in, not since the Reagan era. Too many adverse changes have hit the American workforce in recent decades.

Prosperity Capitalism was brought to an abrupt end; Enrichment Capitalism rose to take its place; average incomes for working Americans stopped rising as they had for an earlier generation.

Economic mismanagement in Washington allowed a major real estate bubble to form in the last years of the Reagan administration, and as the crash followed, working Americans paid the price. Total earnings for working Americans were lower at the end of the George H.W. Bush presidency than they had been at the beginning.

Another round of mismanagement gave America the dotcom bubble and then something of a dotcom crash.

And finally, a badly under-regulated housing market took off on a dangerous boom at the same time that a badly under-regulated banking sector fell in love with "collateralized debt obligations," seemingly safe mortgage securities that were as dangerous as any junk bond. As the real estate bubble came to an end, as the banking system realized how worthless its real estate securities were, the economy crashed, yet again, in the worst downturn since the Great Depression. How are America's working people to save effectively for their retirement when the forces of systemic corruption at the top are so indifferent to their well-being?

In an ideal world, the American economy behaves itself. Jobs are available to everyone. Pay levels rise steadily. And Defined Contribution pension programs work out well for everyone.

In today's world, with systemic corruption entrenched at the top and flattened wages a damaging reality for millions, Defined Contribution pensions are not nearly as beneficial as they could have been. Americans in the Top 30% may be doing all right, but those in the Bottom 70%? Not so good.

Let's turn to Social Security. Social Security worked well when the demographics of the American population were tilted in its favor, with millions of working Americans and not so many retired Americans.

Now that these same demographics are tilting in the opposite direction, what's likely to happen to Social Security? Will Social Security's forecasters show us the way forward? It could happen, I suppose, but I am guessing that it won't. Social Security's experts aren't as wise, alas, as we need them to be.

Why do I say that? Because my own research has shown me that Social Security's solvency yardstick – a formula known as "Actuarial Balance" – is badly mislabeled. In truth, it should more properly be called an Insolvency Yardstick. Its core formula tells us only one thing. Has the program's expected insolvency date been pushed out just a couple inches beyond the edge of Social Security's seventy-five year planning horizon? Any "fix" that postpones Social Security's bankruptcy date till Year 76 or Year 77 will receive a passing grade from those who rely on the Actuarial Balance approach.

I can hear you wondering, "Why on Earth would we want to do that?" My question exactly.

"Actuarial Balance" is one of those non-solution solutions that arise easily in those cultures that don't hold their leaders to exacting standards of craftsmanship. Its continued use reflects a high tolerance for sloppy thinking on the part of Democrats and Republicans alike.

"Actuarial Balance" is not a tool that will ever help our elected leaders develop a responsible answer to the question of how Social Security ought to be restructured for the future.

It might work tolerably well in an America where the ratio between working Americans and retired Americans remained constant, for decades and decades on end.

But in today's demographic environment, the quest for "actuarial balance" will never produce a lasting solution.

For those who follow Social Security closely, it will be remembered that its long-run insolvency challenge was supposedly fixed in 1983 by the Greeenspan Commission, a bipartisan panel of twelve headed by Alan Greenspan and Senator Daniel Patrick Moynihan.

How did they know they had "fixed" Social Security? They "knew," because the program's actuaries had calculated a positive actuarial balance for their proposed reforms. In the carelessness of politics, a proposal scored as producing a positive actuarial balance was taken to be the equivalent of a lasting solution. Alan Greenspan was so sure that he and Moynihan had solved the problem that in his memoir he made a point of bragging about their success.[3]

Let me put the matter to you in cab driver language. Here's what the Greenspan-Moynihan fix in 1983 gave us: "Run a Surplus. Watch the Surplus Disappear. Run a Deficit. Empty out the Trust Fund. Go Broke."

Or in slightly more formal terms, this is the scheme their commission produced: America will grow the Social Security Trust Fund for three or four decades. Then the Trust Fund will stop growing and start to shrink as the Boomer generation retires. In time the Trust Fund will be drawn down to zero. Social Security will be broke and its benefits will have to be cut.

---

3 - Alan Greenspan, The Age of Turbulence. Penguin 2007. p 96.

Yes, this was the Greenspan-Moynihan fix. And Social Security's Actuarial Balance team had given the Greenspan-Moynihan reform package a passing grade.

"Passing grade?" Yes. You want to see it? You can look it up. It's recapped in the 2013 Trustees Report, on page 161, in a table that lists the program's Actuarial Balance forecasts, year-by-year from 1982 through 2013. And, yes, the forecast for 1983 is positive – a passing score.

If we are to develop a lasting fix for Social Security, our first step ought to be obvious. Acknowledge that "Actuarial Balance" is an insolvency yardstick, not a solvency yardstick, and get rid of it. It's inherently unsuited to the demographic challenges of our era. It has to be replaced with a yardstick that genuinely measures lasting solvency.

So how is Social Security to be put on a solid footing – not just for the next three or four decades – but permanently?

Keep in mind, as we wrestle with this problem, that it's a tougher challenge in an era of Enrichment Capitalism than it would be in an era of Prosperity Capitalism. And it's a tougher challenge in a nation dominated by Systemic Corruption than it would be in a nation committed to a politics of Character and Craftsmanship.

Let's start with the rule that defines the size of Social Security's tax base. By law, Social Security taxes are collected on "taxable payroll," so in the end, everything revolves around this as the starting point. "Taxable Payroll" is everything earned that's below a pre-defined cutoff, a Maximum Taxable Earnings cutoff. In 2005, it was $90,000. In 2010, it was $106,800. In 2015, it was $118,500.

In theory, eighty-five percent of what Americans earn is subject to Social Security taxation and fifteen percent is not.

In practice, at least thirty percent of what Americans earn gets exempted.

Let's test this. I will pick one key number out of the Trustees Report for 2014 and another key number out of the Saez database for 2014 and put them side by side.

From the Trustees Report, I calculate Taxable Payroll of $6.2 Trillion.[4]

Then I turn to the Saez database for 2014, in which he shows pretax earnings of $9.1 Trillion.

That's quite a gap. Social Security hasn't collected taxes on eighty-five percent of total earnings for quite some time. The $6.2 Trillion on which it levies Social Security taxes is a long way short of the $9.1 Trillion in pretax earnings that Americans report to the IRS.

Is $9.1 Trillion really the right number? Perhaps not. Some states provide their own government employees with a state-funded alternative to Social Security. So perhaps something a little lower - $8.8 Trillion, perhaps – would be a realistic estimate of the earnings pool on which Social Security taxes could be collected, if we were determined to put the program on a stable footing for decades to come.

Viewed from this perspective, Social Security's insolvency challenge can best be understood as an artifact of its taxable income cutoff policy – the policy that largely shields high-end earnings from Social Security taxation.

But taxing the nation's wealthiest Americans is not the only option that our politicians will want to consider.

One obvious alternative is to trim the benefit formulas on which the retirees of today and tomorrow have been relying. Yes, that's right. In an economy bent on squeezing the poor

---

4 - I use the GDP total from page 203 and I multiply this by "Taxable Payroll as Pct of GDP" from page 205. This calculation shows $6.2 Trillion in taxable payroll.

during their working years, America could achieve savings in its Social Security program by squeezing the elderly even more during their retirement years. This appears to be Paul Ryan's preferred solution.

But is this really the best way to go about it? Protect the earnings of those at the top, who benefit the most from Enrichment Capitalism? Squeeze those at the bottom during their retirement years, after decades of squeezing their employee earnings?

The key point is quite simple. Thirty percent of the nation's pretax income – income that's received by the nation's top earners – is currently shielded from the reach of Social Security taxation. As the nation wrestles with the best way to help its Social Security program achieve lasting solvency, one ought to look first toward the shielded earnings of America's high income elites.

Defined Benefit Pension Programs. Defined Contribution Savings Programs. Social Security. Each has been lauded for its contribution to American retirees, current and future. And yet in none of these areas do we see the sort of sure hands and craftsmanship that ought to be our hallmark.

The Politics of Systemic Corruption will make good solutions harder to find, bad solutions more probable. In our corrupted era, the rich will remain untaxed and Social Security's long-run benefit formulas will be cut.

The path of Character and Craftsmanship would give us a much more honorable solution.

America's
retirement programs are
suffering, partly from
poor craftsmanship, and partly
from a corrupted economy
that's now badly *tilted* against
the **middle class**.

Getting America **UnStuck**
The Politics of **Character** & **Craftsmanship**

americaunstuck.com

★

Chapter Ten

Craftsmanship
THE MEDICAL AFFORDABILITY CHALLENGE

"If it walks like a cartel, and it quacks like a cartel, what is it?"

HERE WE ARE, THE UNITED STATES of America, the nation with the world's most costly medical system, one that soaks up almost 17% of GDP, just as America's senior population is growing at breakneck speed, the nation's wounded veterans are suffering terribly, and diabetes is on the rise.

And here we are, too, trapped within the politics of systemic corruption and held back by a civic culture of gross neglect. Other nations have developed world class solutions to the challenge of delivering universal and affordable medical care, but here in America? We're stuck.

Our times demand wisdom; our politicians reply with cover stories and excuses. We haven't a taste for shaking off systemic corruption, we Americans. Our stuckness appears to be habitual. Alarm bells may be going off, but the public seems numb.

What if we weren't feeling so stuck? What if we were feisty enough to think that we deserve something better? What if we started to apply an ethos of Character and Craftsmanship to our medical sector? What if we were to assess its Character? Get all the way to the bottom of the problem with a rigorous dose of Diagnostic Craftsmanship? And use Prescriptive Craftsmanship to develop a world class solution?

If this were our journey, there are a few things we'd start to notice.

First of all, we'd notice several decades of rising prices, sometimes much faster than GDP growth, sometimes only a shade faster, but hardly ever stable.

Let's do the numbers.[1]

Look to the table below, Figure 10.1.

In Column Two, we see Medical Spending Per Capita, expressed in the dollar values of the day.

In 1960, $147 per person per year for medical care. (1960 dollars).

In 1970, $356 per person per year. (1970 dollars).

In 1980, $1,110 per person per year.

In 1990, $2,855 per person per year.

In 2000, $4,881 per person per year.

In 2010, $8,428 per person per year.

At this rate, by 2020 we'll be at $16,000 per person per year, won't we?

(I should note that price increases in medicine seem to have slowed since the Affordable Care Act was passed.[2])

In Column Three, I use Saez data on average earnings per tax unit to provide a reference point.

---

1 - Source for Column Two: Centers for Medicare & Medicaid Services, Office of the Actuary, National Health Statistics Group; U.S. Department of Commerce, Bureau of Economic Analysis; and U.S. Bureau of the Census: "Table 1 National Health Expenditures; Aggregate and Per Capita Amounts, Annual Percent Change and Percent Distribution: Selected Calendar Years 1960-2013." Sources for Columns Three and Four: Saez database cited above, with constant dollar figures restated as current dollars. Column Five: Author's calculation derived from Columns Two and Four..

2 - Catherine Rampell. "Reports of Obamacare's Demise Are Greatly Exaggerated." The Washington Post. October 13, 2016.

In Column Four, I remove the Top 10%, and I use Saez data on average earnings per tax unit for those in the Bottom 90%. Omitting the wealthy gives us a more meaningful standard of comparison.

And then in Column Five, I show how large the burden of medical care has been relative to average earnings, for each decade from 1960 to 2010. In 1960, for Americans in the Bottom 90%, average per capita medical costs represented only 4.2% of average earnings per tax unit.

By 2010, average per capita medical costs represented almost 29% of average earnings per tax unit. In other words, for lower income Americans, medicine was *seven times more expensive* in 2010 than it had been in 1960.

Fig. 10.1 **MEDICAL SPENDING VS. TAX UNIT EARNINGS 1960 - 2010***				
Year	Medical Spending Per Capita	Average Earnings Per Tax Unit	Average Earnings Per Tax Unit: Bottom 90	Per Capita Spending as Percent of Bottom 90
1960	$147	$4,631	$3,516	4.2%
1970	$356	$8,023	$6,105	5.8%
1980	$1,110	$16,379	$12,218	9.1%
1990	$2,855	$27,949	$18,994	15.0%
2000	$4,881	$42,479	$26,852	18.2%
2010	$8,428	$49,137	$29,220	28.8%

*Current Dollars

Figure 10.1 Medical Spending versus Tax Unit Earnings, 1960 – 2010*

Am I completely comfortable with Saez' current dollar figures for 1960? No. When I think of what my dad earned in 1960, they seem a bit low. And his figures per tax unit in 2010 might also be a little low. (As noted earlier, I'm guessing that the averages in his database are diluted by the presence of part time workers.)

But what we cannot help noticing is the race car growth rate of per capita medical costs over the past half century. The nation's medical sector is now several times more expensive than it was in 1960.

Apply the Character Test. We see the Behaviors (with a capital B). And we see Consequences (with a capital C). If we are to judge the medical sector's Behaviors by their Consequences, can we honestly say to ourselves that this sector functions within the responsibility standards our nation requires?

Apply the Craftsmanship Test. Have the nation's political leaders and corporate leaders crafted a way of providing medical care to the nation that meets world standards? No. With the cost of medical care in America half again as expensive as anybody else's, our medical system plainly flunks the Craftsmanship test as well.

American medicine is a massive example of a cause-and-effect system put together by those of corrupt motives, with little or no regard for the far horizon consequences their systems are likely to produce. How many ashes had they dug out of the incinerator? How many white sheets had they assaulted? It didn't matter. They weren't four year olds. They were corporate bullies. No one in America had the power to hold them accountable, not for their lack of Character, nor for their lack of Craftsmanship.

The best way to explain the ongoing behavior of the nation's medical sector is by pointing to the Politics of Systemic Corruption.

Would our nation spend seventeen percent of its GDP on medical care if the Politics of Character and Craftsmanship were our norm? Of course not. Do we now spend roughly $9,000 per capita on medical care because our political leaders work hand in glove with the forces of Systemic Corruption? Absolutely.

Let's look at this question partly from a diagnostic angle and partly from a prescriptive angle. Our diagnosis is likely to come back with a strong presumption of systemic corruption. And our prescriptive case? Incremental tinkering won't be sufficient. Transformational thinking will be required.

What Sort of Diagnostic Findings Make Sense?

It's Not Just an Industry; It's a Sector. Let's first acknowledge that we're up against the misbehavior of an entire sector. It's a sector that includes the medical insurance industry, the hospital industry, the medical laboratory industry, the pharmaceutical industry, doctors' offices and clinics, medical schools, and even a segment of the nation's lawyers.

Enrichment Capitalism Has Inspired Greed at the Top. Now add Enrichment Capitalism to our story. As we do, we will discover – no surprise – that the nation's medical sector CEOs have been piling on. A quick scan of internet stories about CEO compensation surfaces a series of unsurprising and yet appalling data points from medical insurance corporations, hospital corporations, and pharmaceutical corporations.

Let's begin with medical insurers: Centene's CEO drew $19.3 million in 2014; Aetna's CEO received $15.0 million, and UnitedHealth Group's CEO pulled in $14.9 million.[3]

CEOs of hospital corporations have also been thriving. Community Health System's Wayne Smith received $26.4 million in 2014[4], Hospital Corporation of America's Richard Bracken made $48.2 million in 2012[5], and Tenet Healthcare's Trevor Fetter snared $22.7 million[6].

The same pattern holds for pharmaceutical CEOs. Merck & Company CEO Ken Frazier received $25.0 million in compensation for 2014, while Johnson & Johnson's Alex Gorsky made almost the same amount. Pfizer's Ian Read pulled in $23.3 million in compensation in 2014.[7]

---

3 - Data for all three CEOs from https://aishealth.com/archive/nhpw060115-02

4 - http://www.bloomberg.com/research/stocks/people/person.
    asp?personId=160411&privcapId=26782

5 - http://www.fiercehealthfinance.com/story/healthcare-ceo-pay-skewing-
    economy/2014-06-12

6 - http://www.bizjournals.com/dallas/print-edition/2014/07/04/highest-paid-
    ceos-soleras-tony-aquila-vaults-to.html

7 - http://www.fiercepharma.com/special-reports/top-20-highest-paid-
    biopharma-ceos

Does This Sector Have Customers? Let's ask what may seem to be an off-the- wall question. Does the nation's medical sector have any real customers? As an individual, I may be a "user" of medical care services but I am not the central "payer." I visit a doctor; I sign a credit card slip for my $35 co-pay. Does that make me a "customer" in the traditional sense of the word? I don't think so.

What I pay might be a very small fraction of the total bill. I suffer from macular degeneration, and in my right eye, the disease has progressed to its "wet" stage. Small unwanted blood vessels have begun to form beneath the macula, and if left to themselves, they'd destroy the central portion of my right eye's visual field.

Every eight weeks my eye doctor injects medicine into my right eye in order to halt and reverse blood vessel formation. I wait eight weeks till the medicine in my eyeball dissipates, then we do it again.

Each injection is nominally priced at $3,000; my insurance company reimburses the clinic $2,000 for the medicine and a bit more for the doctor's services. No matter what the cost, though, my copay stays at $35. Two other medicines would have the same medical value, one that's more expensive, and one that's somewhat less expensive. The less costly option is procedurally inconvenient. It would need to be ordered from a compounding pharmacy – an inconvenience for my eye clinic – and administered every four weeks – an inconvenience to me.

My doctor believes the medicine she's using has a slightly better track record, and I like it too because it doesn't entail as many injections per year. Since my money isn't really on the line for any of this, I pick the treatment approach that's the easiest for me – once every eight or nine weeks.

My larger point? The idea that I am a price-sensitive customer simply doesn't correspond to my actual behavior, does it? I am a "user," yes, but am I really a "customer" in the normal sense of the word?

There are three sets of roles that we need to acknowledge – the user, the conduit, and the payer. I'm the user, but I don't really pay. Most of the payment my doctor receives comes from my wife's insurance company (CareFirst BlueChoice, in our case). But CareFirst BlueChoice isn't made of money; it sells policies to employers, and in the final analysis, the money for the care I receive comes from my wife's employer. But does that mean that the employer is "the customer"? Not really. Add the three roles together – The Payer and The Conduit and The User. The Employer and the Insurance Company and the Patient. Are we collectively, "The Customer"? Plainly not. By any conventional standard, the medical sector doesn't have "customers." It has "payers" and "conduits" and "users," yes, but no "customers."

And because there are no customers, by any traditional meaning of the term, there's no price shopping. We bought a new roof for our house and got bids from three roofing companies. We got our house repainted and got bids from seven house painting companies. Have I ever, in my entire life, solicited bids from different doctors? Not that I can recall. I am a medical care "customer" only in the narrowest of ways. There are two pharmacies in my neighborhood. It didn't take me long to figure out which one gives faster service, and that's the one I use. Beyond that, I am not a comparison shopper. Ever.

In the larger meaning of the word "customer", I don't think America's medical sector has customers. It has payers, it has conduits, and it has users. And that's it.

And because it has no customers, who's to enforce price discipline? On the margin, companies that buy medical insurance policies for their employees have some freedom to shop around in hopes of finding a more affordable policy. Individuals who need to buy their own medical insurance policies can go onto a health exchange and engage in modest amounts of comparison shopping. But none of this gives Americans the sort of price leverage that folks in other countries have enjoyed for decades.

Does the Medical Sector Operate as a De Facto Cartel?

So let's ask the next question: Does the U.S. medical sector resemble a monopoly? It's a tempting notion. Barriers to entry are everywhere. It's difficult to get into medical school. It's difficult to launch a new medical school. It's difficult to get licensed to be a doctor. Nurses and other patient care technicians also require extensive training.

Hospitals have to be certified in all sorts of ways. Insurance companies are carefully scrutinized. Unlike hedge funds, one cannot create a pharmaceutical company out of thin air. One might be able to start a medical device company with little more than a good idea, but until the FDA approves the device, the company will have no customers.

In other words, everywhere one looks, one sees entrenched players and high barriers to entry. So, yes, the medical sector smells a bit like a monopoly.

But the medical sector doesn't quite have the powers of coordination and price-fixing that John D. Rockefeller once exercised in the petroleum industry. For all its barriers to entry, it would be an overreach to characterize the U.S. medical sector as a de facto monopoly.

On the other hand, I believe we'd be right on target if we were to characterize the U.S. medical sector as a de facto cartel. Five decades of relentless cartel-like price creep ought to be proof enough. So little price restraint exercised on the part of buyers; so much pricing power at work on the part of sellers; and a powerful economic elite so committed to systemic corruption that its ability to manipulate prices has come to be viewed as a perpetual entitlement. With all these factors and others working in its favor, how could America's medical sector not operate as a price-raising cartel?

It is such a privileged sector. With the mild exception of the medical insurance industry, its players almost never compete on price. In 1960, we Americans spent $147 each on medical care; in 2010, we Americans spent $8,428 apiece on medical care. If it walks like a cartel and it quacks like a cartel, let's not duck the obvious. If we call it a cartel, our diagnosis will be spot on.

Does This Sector Pass the Character Test?

One of the central themes of this book is that we live in a cause-and-effect society, and any system that operates at vast scale will surely have vast consequences. America's medical sector absolutely qualifies. It's a system that operates at enormous scale and it's also a system that produces vast consequences.

In an economy with a Gross Domestic Product of $18 Trillion (in 2015), we Americans find ourselves spending about $3 Trillion for medical care in all its forms.

If our medical sector were run to the same standards as the medical sectors in the rest of the world's industrial nations, medical care in America would cost the nation no more than $2 Trillion a year, if that. In other words, here in America we bear the burden of a trillion dollars a year of waste and profiteering that wouldn't be tolerated in any other industrial nation. Our industrial peers have squeezed out the chronic evils that we still permit.

How does this get rationalized? Politicians and economists will warn us away from the line of inquiry that we ought to use – that it's time to document the cartel-like pricing behaviors of our entire medical sector. They will try to pit free market sentimentality against the brutal economic reality of steeply rising medical costs.

It's the neutered pundit problem. Yet again. It's so much easier to earn a living by rationalizing systemic corruption, so much harder to help the nation find its way toward transformational repair.

But an inquiry into the cartel-like behaviors of American medicine is essential to the larger journey our nation has to take. It's an official inquiry that America desperately needs.

Who suffers from the current system? The rest of the economy suffers. Every company that buys medical insurance for its employees is being charged too much. Lee Iacocca has been widely quoted as saying that automakers pay more for health insurance than they do for steel. With relative medical costs far lower in other countries, American exporters are put at a disadvantage by this sector's ability to rig the prices of nearly everything.

Who suffers? Millions of Americans remain uninsured – not nearly as many as before, thanks to Obamacare, but still far too many. Were our system as sensibly designed as any other modern country's system, almost everyone would be insured. And America's medical system would still be far cheaper than it is today.

Who suffers? America's health results have been slipping relative to the rest of the world. Our problem isn't just a problem of profiteering, it's also a problem of inferior service for the poor. Infant mortality rates are higher, life expectancy is lower.

So, no, America's medical sector cannot be said to pass the Character test. Think millions of freshly washed sheets, hanging on the line but covered with ashes, while no one steps forward to say, "I'm sorry. I shouldn't have tossed ashes all over your clean sheets."

What's worse, given the Systemic Corruption by which this sector defends its special privileges, is that honest debate is impossibly difficult. This sector unleashes squadrons of crooked propagandists to prey on our fears every time the issue of responsible reform is put on the table.

It is not a sector that's willing to entertain an open and thoughtful consideration of the different business models we might consider, and the means by which cause-and-effect choices already made by others could help us succeed in similar ways here in America. This sector wants us – the American electorate – to be so wary of this debate that we'd rather turn it off than endure the din of a thousand screaming propagandists.

America's medical sector is not just corrupt in a quiet, laugh-all-the-way-to-the-bank sort of way. It's corrupt in an evil, dishonest, bullying, and lying sort of way. It's corrupt in a "Buying up all the politicians it can" sort of way. It's corrupt in a "Keep America Permanently Stuck" sort of way. It's corrupt in a "We Hate Character and We Hate Craftsmanship" sort of way.

That being said, Character is essential, no matter how much ill-gotten wealth the medical sector might wish to expend in hopes of getting us to think otherwise. This sector's overall business model has become far too corrupt and expensive to endure; it will be an essential act of good Character for us to say so.

What Sort of Prescriptive Recommendations Make Sense?

Figuring out an honorable, effective, and affordable business model for America's medical sector is a Really Hard Problem. I don't think we can wave a wand, as Bernie Sanders would love to do, utter the words, "Cover everyone with Medicare," and imagine that the prescriptive craftsmanship will flow down on us like waters.

The world likes to present us with two kinds of really hard problems. Some really hard problems have never been solved before, not by anyone. And some have.

The problem of inventing the world's first airplane was a really hard problem that nobody had ever solved before. Orville and Wilbur Wright had to figure out their own answers to a long series of unsolved challenges. Every summer for three years, they traveled from Dayton, Ohio, to Kill Devil Hills on North Carolina's outer banks to test the experimental aircraft they had built. (They loved the steady winds at Kill Devil Hills; those winds gave their gliders lots of extra air speed.) In 1901, their theories about flight were still too flawed; their gliders kept crashing. Discouraged, they momentarily imagined that they'd have to give up their dream. But within a few months, fresh ideas had come and they had found solutions to a series of "what's missing?" challenges.

In 1902, they returned to Kill Devil Hills with a redesigned glider, launched themselves into the wind time and again, and learned in a long succession of glider flights how to tweak their aircraft and fly it successfully.

Finally, in 1903, with all that experience under their belts, they came back with a powered glider, a plane with an engine and a propeller. They gave it a go. Their first powered flight barely went 100 feet. The second went 200 feet. The third flight covered 300 feet. And their fourth flight stayed aloft for more than 800 feet. With this, Wilbur and Orville became so excited they forgot to tie down their plane. Oof! A gust of wind picked it up, flipped it, and damaged it. No more flying for the moment. They hiked off to the telegraph office in Kitty Hawk and sent a victory telegram to their dad.

The problem of learning how to operate a diesel engine manufacturing company at world class standards was also a Really Hard Problem, for Cummins, but at least for Cummins it was a problem that someone else had already solved. The folks at Cummins didn't have to start from scratch, but they did have to figure out what their rivals already knew, then teach themselves to replicate those skills inside the company and across their entire supply chain.

The problem of figuring out how to organize an effective and affordable medical sector is hard, but it's not hard in a Wright Brothers way. It's hard in a Cummins sort of way. Other nations – more than twenty – have already worked out solutions that outperform America's medical sector.

So it won't be quite as hard, in an intellectual sense, as some folks claim.

What will make it hard is a trillion dollars a year of over-pricing. What will make it hard are the Politics of Systemic

Corruption. What will make it hard is the reluctance of the American public to press for transformational change even in circumstances of great duress.

Whose approach do we admire the most? If we were to pick one nation that seems to have done the best job, one nation whose approach we would most like to copy, which nation would that be? What would make it special? And how might we tweak it before we make it our own?

T.R. Reid, in *The Healing of America*, recounts his experiences as a patient with an ailing shoulder, visiting the medical systems of Canada, England, France, Germany, India, and Japan in search of an effective treatment. He tells the story in a way that makes it both accessible and also illuminating for Americans who think that comparison-shopping is always a good idea.[8]

And that was Reid's aim. He saw himself as a comparison-shopping journalist, if you will, seeking to learn all he could from six exemplary countries so that he might give American readers a substantive awareness of the different models on offer. He invites the reader to share his journey and consider his appraisals of each country's strong points and weak points.

Reid's skills as a journalist make this an excellent introduction to the topic of how different countries go about organizing their medical systems. Reid finds three broad options for us to consider.

(1) The Public Insurer/Public Provider System - England's model.

(2) The Public Insurer/Private Provider System – Canada's model, widely known as a Single Payer System.

---

7 - T.R. Reid. *The Healing of America: A Global Quest for Better, Cheaper, and Fairer Health Care.* The Penguin Press. 2009.

---

(3) The Private Insurer/Private Provider Systems – France, Germany, and many others.

All three systems experience the pressure of rising costs. Each country finds its own approach, but when everything is said and done, cost control can be achieved through limits placed on total service, or through limits placed on price, or both.

In a system that regulates the *quantity* of service to be performed, not every request for surgery will get approved.

In a system that regulates the *prices* to be charged, every chargeable service is given a fixed price and no one gets to charge more.

The Brits are more willing than most to limit services. Yes, it creates frictions with the public, and is one of the central reasons the British model isn't likely to be the one we'd seek to emulate here.

In Reid's telling, though, there are more examples in which countries control total spending by controlling prices. The French control prices. The Germans control prices. In Reid's view, the Japanese were the most ferocious. Their price schedule was so tight that Reid began to worry about the relentlessly spartan furnishings of Japan's medical clinics. Yet – from a budget point of view – Japan's approach works well, holding medical costs to just above ten percent of GDP, quite an accomplishment given its expanding retiree population.

In Germany, the process of setting prices is characterized by Reid as being somewhat tense. Providers push for higher charges; the government feels honor bound to keep the entire system affordable.

Reid's treatment of the French system doesn't focus on this issue. Of all the countries Reid visited, France seemed to him to have both the happiest doctors and the happiest patients. Who can say how accurate this may be, but his book left me thinking that the French model might be the one from which we have the most to learn.

But there's more to the story Reid tells than a willingness to keep medicine affordable by controlling prices.

In the countries Reid visited, government-subsidized medical school was a common theme. It makes sense. Think, for a moment, about the signal given to future doctors in today's America. Text: "As you earn your MD, you will find yourself going deeply into debt." Subtext: "You will pay off your debts by charging high fees for your services. Medicine in America is about getting rich. That's why government lets you pay your own way through medical school."

It's a shortsighted strategy on two counts. Not only does it produce a professional work force that's out to gouge its patients, it also creates a mismatch between the kind of doctors America needs and the kind of doctors that America produces. We *need* geriatric doctors; we *don't produce* geriatric doctors. Result – lots of old people, not nearly enough geriatric doctors. It turns out that markets often aren't as smart as some people pretend they are. That's one of the reasons we have government – to notice the gaps that markets create and to get those gaps filled.

There's another large piece of the nation's medical sector that other countries handle more wisely. In Germany, for example, medical insurance isn't set up on a for-profit basis; medical insurance companies by law operate as non-profits. All insurers offer the same plans, at the same prices, to all comers. Some end up with older and sicker clients; others are lucky enough to have younger and healthier clients. Some insurers end the year with losses, others end the year with profits, and then there's a settling up. The goal is to have all companies break even. Those that come out ahead throw their surpluses in a common pool; those that come out behind cover their losses by making withdrawals from that pool.

In such a system, two armies of claims processing clerks disappear. One army of clerks works in doctor's offices and hospitals; the other army works for the medical insurance companies. When all policies provide identical coverage and when all prices are pre-determined, the role of the processing clerk disappears.

But one may wonder. If medical insurance has to be run on a non-profit basis, why would anybody want to handle it? Reid's answer: Medical insurance isn't the heart of anyone's business model, it's just a service provided by insurers who offer a range of other products. They win customers by selling them medical insurance policies, and then they cross-sell. Homeowner's insurance. Auto insurance. Life insurance. The rest of their portfolio is for-profit. Only medical insurance is set up on a not-for-profit basis. Reid flags this as one of the keys to the cost advantage other countries enjoy.

Embrace the Politics of Character and Craftsmanship and we will have an easier time appraising the cause-and-effect forces shaping American medicine today and the consequences they produce.

A commitment to Character compels us to weigh the significance of what we see. Does the present business model of American medicine meet honorable standards? Or has it become a source of systemic damage? Today's system is known for its service gaps and its overpricing.

If the principle of good Character is used to test the business models that shape American medicine, odds are we'll judge that it fails the Character test.

This would lead us into a journey of Diagnostic Craftsmanship. Does this sector function like a cartel? Does it damage the nation and the American people? Can the business decisions that shaped this sector in the past withstand critical scrutiny? Has it gotten too comfortable within a business model that's far inferior to most of America's peers? Do its shortcomings damage the American people? Do they damage the well-beng of our nation as a whole?

From there we would soon find ourselves facing the challenge of Prescriptive Craftsmanship. This is more than a question of "what's good enough?" This is a question of "what's the best possible way of handling this challenge?" It's much the same question Cummins encountered. "Who does it best? What can we learn from them? How can we redefine our way of doing business so that in time we'll be just as effective as they are?" For Cummins, this was a bracing journey. And for America's medical sector, a similar journey could also become a bracing journey.

It could well become a journey guided by a transformational vision ("let's wind up with a system at least as good as the one in France") but put together as a journey of step-by-step change. Take each step carefully. Make sure each step works properly. Then take the next step.

As with Cummins, where the journey to Six Sigma quality took the form of incremental adjustments, one after another, until the entire supply chain had dramatically raised its game, the journey to an honorable, affordable, and effective business model for medicine will almost surely be a journey of small steps, all guided by a wiser vision and a deep spirit of craftsmanship.

At the core of this journey, I predict we will find ourselves saying something new. I predict we will find ourselves reaching higher than we first thought we would. If it's time to go to all the trouble of changing core practices in the nation's medical sector, why settle for "just good enough"? Surely we would want to finish the journey knowing that America had developed one of the best business models in the world for its medical sector.

After all, a spirit of "being just good enough" was how we got ourselves stuck in the first place. We'd want to end up being "as good as the best." If we're going to go to the trouble of reworking our business model, let's take it on in a spirit of aiming as high as we can.

An aspirational America won't sit still for the idea that "being just good enough" is all that matters. There's more to us than that. Let's commit ourselves to top-notch craftsmanship and become the best of which we are capable.

In **1960**, medical care cost us
$147 a year each.
In **2010** it cost us $8,437 a year
apiece. Whodunit?

America's Medical Sector.

*It if walks like a cartel and it
quacks like a cartel, it's a cartel.*

Chapter Eleven

Craftsmanship
THE GLOBAL WARMING CHALLENGE

"Not just another emission cleanup problem."

LOOK IN ANY DIRECTION. AMERICA FALLS SHORT. Schools? We haven't been curious enough to discover their full possibilities. Economic inequality? Only a symptom – the real problem is much deeper. Pensions and Social Security? Behind the curve, yet again. Medical costs? Way too steep, and we have yet to name the problem for what it really is.

And what about our response to global warming? Have we fallen short here as well? Sadly, yes.

As a nation we are mostly but not completely stuck, in an underlying reality that combines an unpleasant mix of corruption and carelessness. Corruption from players in the fossil fuel industry and the politicians they support, yes. And carelessness from scientists and environmentalists who imagine themselves to be the voice of change. Industry wants us to pretend the problem isn't real. Activists want us to pretend that the problem is simple enough to be squeezed into soundbites and tackled with simplistic slogans, angry demonstrations, and human barricades.

There's been far too little Character on the part of industry, and far too little Craftsmanship on the part of the reformers.

As with so many other issues, our diagnostic craftsmanship hasn't been sharp enough to take us to the heart of the challenge;

our prescriptive craftsmanship has been too timid to point us toward a full solution.

We cannot get where we need to go by staying on the road we are currently following. We will have to overcome the casual habits of the past if we are to develop the craftsmanship this threat demands.

So let's restart the conversation. It will be the easiest way. In this chapter I will illustrate a more careful diagnostic approach; in the next chapter I will propose a higher prescriptive standard.

Global warming is one of those complex issues that should never have been reduced to a single soundbite, and yet that's exactly what happened. Our scientific and environmental leaders warned us that global warming was real, an "emissions reduction" problem that would require us to be more prudent in our use of fossil fuels.

"Emission Reduction" was never the right message. To understand why, it's best to start by acknowledging the full sequence of cause-and-effect relationships that have produced this crisis:

A. We inherit from history a vast portfolio of energy technologies that rely on fossil fuels.

B. The more we use these technologies, the more fossil fuels we burn and the more CO_2 emissions we leave in our wake.

C. The more emissions we produce, the more we raise the total stock of atmospheric CO_2.

D. An ever-growing stock of atmospheric CO_2 causes ongoing global warming.

E. The warmer the Earth becomes, the more dangerous its climate becomes.

That's the larger cause-and-effect setting in which we find ourselves. Yes, global warming is directly caused by rising concentrations of CO_2 in the atmosphere, but it doesn't follow that we are to cure this threat by promoting "emission reductions" as though that would be enough.

And while we speak of "global warming" as the threat to be managed, it's clear that our culture has but the vaguest idea of the full peril that lies ahead. We are in much greater danger from the intensification of climate extremes than we are from the steady climb in average temperatures.

None of these confusions can be cured through intra-mural arguments over which soundbite works best, or by quarreling about which shortcut to a full solution has the best chance of turning out thousands of demonstrators.

Until we take in the totality of our situation, we won't be able to appreciate the sort of civic responsibility that this crisis has imposed on our generation.

So let's start at the beginning, with our fuels and the technologies they require.

A. Today's technology portfolio forces our dependence on fossil fuels.

It's no mystery to anyone that our civilization has become heavily dependent on its energy technologies and the fossil fuels that power them. Our buildings are largely (but not entirely) warmed with heating oil and natural gas. Our cars are powered with gasoline, our eighteen-wheelers, trains, and ocean freighters with diesel fuel, and our airplanes with aviation and jet fuel. Industry consumes prodigious quantities of oil and natural gas. Our electricity is generated partly from nuclear power, partly from hydropower and wind, but significantly – still – from the burning of natural gas and coal. Our fossil fuel technologies turn us into consumers of fossil fuels.

B. The more fossil fuels we burn, the more CO_2 emissions we produce.

When we burn hydrocarbons of any kind (coal, oil, natural gas), we produce exhaust molecules of oxidized hydrogen (H_2O), also known as water vapor, and exhaust molecules of oxidized carbon (CO_2), also known as carbon dioxide.

Humanity's dependence on fossil fuels produces a staggering amount of consumption and a staggering amount of CO_2 exhaust. Across the planet, our total consumption of fossil fuels leads to thirty-five billion metric tonnes of carbon dioxide exhaust every year.[1] There's a bit more to the global warming problem than carbon dioxide, but it is much the largest part. [A "metric tonne" of CO_2 refers to a thousand kilograms of CO_2, roughly 2,205 pounds.]

C. Carbon dioxide emissions cause the stock of atmospheric CO_2 to rise.

Of each year's CO_2 emissions, a portion will be absorbed by the world's woodlands. Another portion will be absorbed by the world's oceans and seas with much of it turned into carbonic acid. Finally, the remainder – about half of the world's CO_2 emissions – will join the CO_2 already in the atmosphere, driving even higher the atmosphere's total concentration of CO_2.

Scientists measure CO_2 emissions in metric tonnes; they measure atmospheric CO_2 in Parts Per Million by volume (PPM). This disparity can be confusing, so at one point I tracked down a scientist able to tell me the conversion factor. One PPM of carbon dioxide weighs 7.77 billion tonnes,[2] which tells us that a rise of 2 PPM per year means that roughly 16 billion tonnes of carbon dioxide get added to the total stock of atmospheric CO_2 every year.

---

1 - http://edgar.jrc.ec.europa.eu/news_docs/jrc-2014-trends-in-global-co2-emissions-2014-report-93171.pdf, p. 11

2 - Conversion ratio supplied in personal email from T.J. Blasing of Oak Ridge National Laboratories, 2006-09-15.

Scientists now know – thanks to what they've learned from all the ice cores they've extracted from Greenland and Antarctica – that the atmosphere's baseline level for CO_2 was 280 Parts Per Million. Then the Industrial Revolution got under way. Coal had an early lead, but petroleum and natural gas soon became just as vital. At today's concentration of 400 PPM (and climbing), atmospheric CO_2 is presently 43% higher than it was throughout quite a long stretch of human history. The era of fossil fuels is a relatively recent feature of human history; only in the late 1700s would this new era begin to pump new CO_2 into the atmosphere.

Even a century ago, some scientists suspected that atmospheric CO_2 levels were rising, but no one knew for sure. The most well-known worrier, Alexander Graham Bell, had already guessed in 1917 that the consumption of fossil fuels could lead to global warming. [3]

As industrialization made its way into more and more parts of the world, with the inevitable burning of more and carbon fuels, the question of what this meant attracted a rising level of scientific attention. Were CO_2 levels rising, or were they not? If the atmosphere wasn't taking on more CO_2, where was it going instead?

It was a serious question, and it deserved a serious answer. In 1958, U.S. scientists established the world's first carbon dioxide observatory, atop Mauna Loa in the middle of the Pacific. For all Mauna Loa's scenic cachet, the point was to measure CO_2 concentrations in a location so distant from industry that the observatory's numbers would be accepted by everyone as reasonable approximations of the global average.

---

3 - (From Wikipedia) Surtees, Lawrence (2005). "Bell, Alexander Graham". In Cook, Ramsay; Bélanger, Réal. *Dictionary of Canadian Biography*. XV (1921–1930) (online ed.). University of Toronto Press. Also Grosvenor, Edwin S. and Morgan Wesson. *Alexander Graham Bell: The Life and Times of the Man Who Invented the Telephone*. New York: Harry N. Abrahms, Inc., 1997, p. 274, ISBN 0-8109-4005-1.

With their initial measurements in 1958, America's scientists learned that CO_2 was present in the atmosphere at a concentration of 315 Parts Per Million. At first they wondered if that was to be a stable measurement or if it would climb over time. It wasn't long before they had their answer. CO_2 was indeed on the rise. From 1958 to 1968, CO_2 concentration climbed by 8 PPM. From 1968 to 1978, they climbed by 12 PPM. From 1978 to 1988, they climbed by 16.6 PPM. From 1988 to 1998, they climbed by another 15.6 PPM. From 1998 to 2008, it climbed by another 18.5 PPM. The accumulation rate has been bumpy but it has clearly been intensifying.

Once in the atmosphere, new CO_2 hasn't much of anywhere else to go. The natural processes that remove CO_2 from the atmosphere operate over very long time scales. Even if by magic one could halt all further emissions of CO_2, its atmospheric concentration would decline quite slowly.

D. An ever-growing stock of atmospheric CO_2 causes ongoing global warming

The greater the total amount of CO_2 the atmosphere acquires, the higher the Earth's average temperature will become.

This is really heart of the matter – the cause-and-effect link that ties the total amount of CO_2 in the atmosphere to planet Earth's natural equilibrium temperature. The higher the stock of atmospheric stock of CO_2, the higher the Earth's equilibrium temperature. The lower the stock of CO_2, the lower the Earth's equilibrium temperature. (Scientists sometimes refer to this concept as "heat balance.")

There are two other factors that need to be noted – long-run changes in the Earth's orbit, indirectly caused by Jupiter's gravitational influence, and the potential for regional changes, especially in northern Europe, that will take place if the Gulf Stream intensifies or quiets down.

The long-run orbital shifts are called Milankovitch cycles, after the Serbian scientist who identified their existence in the

1940s. There are three sets of periodic cycles that interact. At one of their cyclic extremes, they produce very cold winters for the northern hemisphere and set off new ice ages. At the other cyclic extreme, they produce warmer winters that cause ice ages to come to an end. As its ice sheets melt, the Earth transitions into what scientists refer to as its "inter-glacial" periods.

And that's where we are now, in the middle of an inter-glacial period. We are still some thousands of years away from the orbital shifts that could plunge the Earth back into its next ice age.

Once an ice age gets under way, the Earth's oceans become much colder, and just as an ice cold soda holds more fizz than a warm soda, very cold oceans take up more carbon dioxide from the atmosphere than warmer oceans. Ice core measurements that go back as much as eight hundred thousand years show atmospheric CO_2 falling to 180 Parts Per Million during the Earth's ice ages, then rising to 280 Parts Per Million during inter-glacial periods.[4]

(Another factor that's capable of altering the climate is the Gulf Stream. Shifts in the Gulf Stream won't have global impacts, but they can cause continental Europe to swing between warmer periods and cooler periods. Let's set this issue to the side, as it isn't something that we humans affect.)

Today's global warming represents a further boost to the generally warm temperatures that accompany any inter-glacial period.

Today, with carbon dioxide levels rising by 2 Parts Per Million every year, it's clear that our civilization is running an uncontrolled experiment on how a major shift in a key climate variable will affect the entire Earth. How much added warming will the Earth experience as a result of all the carbon dioxide that human action has pumped into the atmosphere? And

---

4 - http://cdiac.ornl.gov/trends/co2/ice_core_co2.html

what sort of consequences will follow in its wake? Talk about Actions on a vast scale, and Consequences on a vast scale, and the question of whether we humans will accept Responsibility for our Actions and for the Consequences they generate.

The risks are real. The risk probabilities are serious. But before considering those risks, let's acquaint ourselves with the cause-and-effect processes that our actions have set in motion.

Step One – The Default Situation. Two distinct flows of energy are continuously involved in shaping the Earth's average temperature – Energy IN and Energy OUT. The sun's energy arrives continually – Energy IN. Some of the sun's energy arrives in the ultraviolet portion of the spectrum, some arrives in the visible light portion of the spectrum, and some arrives in the near infrared portion of the spectrum. Wavelengths for sunlight in this part of the spectrum are measured in microns (a millionth of a meter) and in fractions of a micron.

The other flow of energy – Energy OUT – is generated by the Earth. Think of the infrared spectrum. Warm bodies glow more brightly in an infrared viewer than cool bodies, and what's true for humans trying to flee from police helicopters at night is also true for the Earth as a whole as it speeds through space. Warm parts of the planet glow more brightly, and all parts of the planet, however warm or cool they may be, play a part in radiating infrared energy away from the Earth and out into space.

Both of these flows are continuous. Energy IN from the sun arrives 24 hours a day, albeit only on the side of the Earth then turned toward the sun. Energy OUT leaves the Earth as an infrared glow of differing intensities, and it flows into space from all parts of the Earth, day and night alike.

Now to the key point. Under normal conditions, these two flows of energy stay in balance. On its daylight side, the Earth receives Energy IN from the sun; on both its daylight side and its night-time side, the Earth radiates Energy OUT off into space.

Energy OUT cools the Earth. Our planet sheds its excess heat by radiating infrared energy out into space.

Energy IN warms the Earth. Our planet receives heat from all the sunlight that comes its way.

If the Earth is to experience a steady average temperature, over the course of a year or a decade or even a century, what has to be true? Energy OUT has to offset Energy IN, right? The energy that the Earth dumps into space has to offset, fully, the energy that the Earth has received from the sun. This balancing is a continuous process, and under normal conditions it keeps the Earth at an equilibrium temperature. The 1800s were roughly the same temperature as the 1600s because in both centuries, Energy IN from the Sun was fully offset by Energy OUT, the earthshine that our planet sends back into space.

Think of it this way. My car has a cooling system; its radiator gets rid of the extra heat that's been generated by the engine. Dogs have natural cooling systems; they get rid of excess heat by panting. Humans have a natural cooling system; we get rid of excess heat by sweating.

And the Earth, too, has a natural cooling system. It maintains a steady temperature by sending just as much energy out into space, using infrared photons, as it receives from the sun, in the form of higher intensity photons.

You might not have given this any thought. It is so built into the way the Earth works that only a trained scientist is likely to notice its presence. Your morning weather forecaster could care less. She won't spend a nickel's worth of time explaining the Earth's natural cooling system to her viewers.

Step Two. Let's do a thought experiment. Suppose we were able to take away some of the atmosphere's greenhouse gases. Take away carbon dioxide. Take away water vapor. Take away methane. And so on.

What would happen?

Energy OUT would rise. Why? Because a higher percentage of

the Earth's infrared energy would make a full journey through the atmosphere, past all the molecules of greenhouse gas, and into outer space. Any gas known as a greenhouse gas has the ability to intercept photons of infrared energy and bounce them back toward the Earth's surface. Molecules of a greenhouse gas are a bit like bumpers in a pinball game – except that they'll intercept photons, bounce them back toward the Earth, and prevent their escape from the Earth's atmosphere.

So, in this thought experiment, if the atmosphere's supply of greenhouse gases were to fall, more of the Earth's infrared glow would get radiated away into space. In other words, Energy OUT would rise.

What about Energy IN? Its level would stay constant. Greenhouse gases have little or no effect on the amount of sunshine the Earth receives.

With no change in the Earth's warming radiation from the sun, and a noticeable increase in the amount of infrared energy escaping into space, the Earth would cool. It would shed old heat faster than it receives new heat.

This imbalance wouldn't last, though. As the Earth cooled, its output of infrared energy would shrink. Energy OUT would weaken, while Energy IN remained constant. A cooler equilibrium temperature would take hold, lower and cooler than the previous equilibrium temperature.

Scientists would speak of this as "Heat Balance," the condition under which the Earth arrives at its "Equilibrium Temperature."

Step Three. In Step Two, we imagined a decline in the Earth's greenhouse gases. Now, for Step Three, let's visualize the reverse – an increase in the concentration of greenhouse gases in the Earth's atmosphere.

How are we to think about the dynamics that this sort of shift would produce?

Let's go back to the pinball analogy. Just as a reduction in greenhouse gas is analogous to a reduction in the number of bumpers that your pinball has to dodge, an increase in greenhouse gas is analogous to an increase in the number of bumpers ready to interfere with your pinball. Your pinball, i.e. your photon of infrared energy, is desperate to make it all the way to the edge of the Earth's atmosphere without being blocked, and from there to shoot onward into space. That's what infrared photons do. They flee the Earth's atmosphere and dump the Earth's unwanted heat into the far reaches of outer space.

And that's what they'll want to do, even as we add more and more carbon dioxide to the atmosphere. Even as we create more obstacles for all those photons of infrared energy. And we'll succeed. By adding greenhouse gases to the atmosphere, we'll decrease the flow of photons that make their way to outer space.

Energy OUT will therefore shrink.

An imbalance will emerge. Thanks to the sun, Energy IN will remain roughly the same, even as the flow of Energy OUT gets reduced. What served as a stable equilibrium temperature earlier, before all those greenhouse gases got pumped into the atmosphere, won't serve as a stable temperature any longer. The Earth will warm. And as it warms, its flow of infrared photons will intensify. Energy OUT will rise because the Earth as a whole is getting warmer.

In other words, the only way for the Earth to regain its thermal equilibrium is to get warmer.

If the increase in greenhouse gases is a one-time thing, the Earth will regain its Heat Balance, not at yesterday's cooler temperature, but at tomorrow's warmer temperature, and then its temperature will level off. No further change in greenhouse gas, no further change in the Earth's equilibrium temperature.

Step Four. In Step Three, we added a new dose of CO_2 (or other greenhouse gas) and then we stopped. The Earth got warmer, and then its temperature stabilized.

In Step Four, we will make one more adjustment to our thought experiment. We will add new CO_2 on a continuous basis. Every day the total concentration of greenhouse gases will be higher than it was the day before. Every day, these gases will interfere with the Earth's natural cooling system just a little more ferociously than before.

What will this new situation look like?

Energy OUT will shrink. At any given equilibrium temperature for the Earth, its outbound flow of photons will get choked back. Too many bumper added to the pinball machine. Too many ways for outbound photons to get bounced back to the surface. The flow of outbound photons won't be able to carry away as much energy as before. The heat that they sought to remove from the Earth will end up staying put. The Earth will slowly warm, and its infrared intensity will slowly rise, but even as it does, a rising concentration of greenhouse gas will continue to depress the total energy the Earth sheds into outer space.

In the scenario where the total amount of greenhouse gas in the atmosphere rises steadily, the temperature at which the Earth can reestablish its equilibrium will creep up as well.

Think of a car radiator that's slowly losing its efficiency.

The more our experiment interferes with the Earth's natural cooling system, the more we can expect the Earth's average temperature to creep upward. Day by day, month by month, decade by decade.

On a daily basis, the warming we generate will be almost imperceptible – perhaps one twenty-thousandth of a degree. But what if we measure the new temperature every ten years instead of every day?

It's likely we'll notice the rise – roughly a sixth of a degree Celsius with every passing decade. And it won't just be warmer in the atmosphere. The Earth's oceans will be warmer. The Earth's land areas will be warmer. The heat that our experiment traps inside the atmosphere doesn't disappear every evening –

it accumulates, and accumulates, and accumulates.

As you can tell, I have just explained global warming. If the atmosphere is something of a pinball machine, as experienced by infrared photons trying to make their getaway, the more CO_2 those photons encounter, the more they'll be bounced back to the Earth's surface. The flow of Energy OUT won't keep up with the flow of Energy IN, and because it won't, the Earth will slowly get warmer.

The more CO_2 the atmosphere acquires, in other words, the greater the gap we'll have created between Energy IN and Energy OUT. Choking off the Earth's natural cooling system will inevitably produce an overheated Earth, just as tying a dog's mouth shut to prevent the dog from panting would inevitably produce an overheated dog.

As you know, this isn't really a thought experiment, involving hypothetical greenhouse gases being added to the hypothetical atmosphere of a hypothetical planet.

This is a natural experiment, involving a real planet, a real atmosphere, and real human beings who consume real fossil fuels every day, thereby generating massive amounts of carbon dioxide exhaust every single day. Our energy corporations extract carbon from deep in the Earth and humans all over the planet burn it. The greater our cumulative consumption, the greater the atmosphere's carbon dioxide overload.

Energy IN remains the same. Energy OUT gets suppressed. And the Earth warms, slowly but inexorably, as the total stock of atmospheric CO_2 rises.

Now let's ask ourselves what we can learn from this.

In the early years of scientific and environmental worries about this trend and the threat it poses, it was common to see the question framed with an image borrowed from the days of the Clean Air Act. Factory emissions had polluted the air in cities all over the world. Reformers argued for cleaner air and for regulations that would compel factories to reduce their dirty emissions. And it had worked. Urban air stopped being as dirty as it had been.

It was logical – or it seemed logical – to think of global warming in similar terms. Just as emission regulations had tamed the earlier problem, why not use another round of emission regulations to bring this new emissions problem under control?

And from this thought the world ended up with the "emission reduction" logic that shaped international discussions on this challenge. The reformers made what they thought was a logical argument. Get every nation to agree to a significant amount of emission reductions and we'd bring the problem under control. An emission reduction strategy had worked once before; why not use it again?

Let's go back to the core standard called for in this book. Let's become a society of good character; let's accept responsibility for the cause-and-effect systems of modern society and for the consequences they create.

So far, so good. The scientists and environmentalists of that era had called for the world, in a show of good character, to accept responsibility for its carbon dioxide emissions and for the adverse consequences they produce.

But what about the next step? The commitment to Diagnostic Craftsmanship?

This is where our specialists failed miserably.

It had been true, in our polluted cities, that polluted emissions produced polluted air, and that regulatory controls on those emissions would clean up the air.

But it wasn't true that global warming was a function of each year's emissions. The diagnostic call was badly blown.

You already know enough to know why. What matters to global warming *is the total stock of atmospheric CO_2*. The greater the CO_2 overload, the greater the eventual warming. Even if the reformers had been able to flip a switch and turn off all further emissions of CO_2, the Earth would have remained on a warming trajectory for some time to come. With its significantly higher stocks of atmospheric CO_2, their warming effects would have continued until the Earth had settled into its new temperature equilibrium, in a somewhat warmer state than before.

The Kyoto Protocol had been rationalized by the cause-and-effect argument that global warming is caused by carbon dioxide emissions. That assumption was always wrong – irresponsibly wrong – and the basic framework of Kyoto was always wrong as well.

We live in a cause and effect world, remember? If the goal was to end up with a complete halt to global warming, the world was going to have to set a firm cap on the total amount of CO_2 that it would allow itself to dump into the atmosphere.

Even from the very beginning, that's how the goal should have been framed. This issue should always have been framed in a precise, cause-and-effect statement of the effects to be achieved and the actions that would be required.

If the effect to be achieved was a complete halt to global warming, only a halt to all further emissions of CO_2 would have been able to accomplish that aim.

Let's recognize our error now. The world's diagnosticians blew their assignment. They misread the cause-and-effect situation, explained it inaccurately to the world as a whole, and pointed hundreds of millions in somewhat the wrong direction.

The core cause-and-effect reality remains. The more carbon dioxide the atmosphere accumulates, the warmer the Earth becomes.

There is one more step in this series of cause-and-effect links – the one that connects the amount of global warming we get to the amount of climate change we get.

E. The higher the Earth's temperature, the more dangerous its climate becomes

Lots of folks speak casually of "global warming" and "climate change" as though they were two different terms for the same thing.

This is a serious, high risk error, one that needs to be set aside at the earliest possible date.

A number of cause-and-effect logic steps have brought us to this point. What we have seen, with the first four steps, are forces of proportionality at work. Read each of the following with an eye to proportionality.

- The consumption of fossil fuels is roughly proportional to the total number of energy-burning gadgets we own. The more fossil fuel gadgets we load up with, the more fossil fuels we will burn.

- Humanity's emissions of carbon dioxide are proportional to the amount of fossil fuel we consume.

- The total CO_2 overload in the atmosphere is proportional to humanity's cumulative emissions of CO_2.

- The total rise in the Earth's temperature is roughly proportional to the growing overload of carbon dioxide.

So far, so good. Rules of proportionality seem to hold at every step. Can we expect climate change to intensify in roughly the same manner?

Without thinking too hard about it, most folks would probably say "Yes." The more warming we have, the more climate change we'll have. Aren't we still in a world of proportionality?

Let's *not* make that leap.

This, too, is where even our smartest climate scientists have permitted themselves a risky dose of careless thinking. Why not treat "global warming" and "climate change" as two names for roughly the same thing?

Does that actually happen? Indeed it does.

Let me show you what I mean. Let's turn our attention to a formula that has become ingrained among climate scientists, a formula called the "climate sensitivity formula." Like any good formula, it mathematically links an independent variable to a dependent variable, and it provides a fast and convenient way of answering a simple question.

Here's the question: For a given increase in carbon dioxide increase, how much of a temperature increase can the world expect?

By rights, a formula that answers this question ought to be called a *"Temperature Sensitivity Formula,"* because that's what it describes, the sensitivity of the Earth's temperature to the atmosphere's stock of CO_2.

But that's not how scientists speak of this formula. They speak of it as a *Climate Sensitivity Formula,* a habit that implicitly treats "temperature" and "climate" as two different names for the same thing.

Is this wise? I don't think so.

Yes, *rising temperatures* as a function of *rising carbon dioxide* will follow rules of proportionality.

But does it therefore follow that the intensity of future climate change will be proportionally linked to future amounts of *temperature change?* There's very little reason to think that it will, and plenty of reasons to think that it won't.

I think we already know that small shifts in *temperature* can and do produce large shifts in *climate.*

With climate, what matters most are its extremes. Jim Hansen has argued this point by using bell curves, and asking his readers to reflect on what happens to the extreme edge of a severe weather bell curve as the Earth's average temperature inches upward.

In an earlier era, very extreme storms would have been at least five standard deviations to the right of the norm. The very worst scenarios almost never happened.

Now, Hansen notes, picture the entire bell curve inching slowly to the right as the Earth warms. Events that would have been five standard deviations to the right, in the world's more temperate past, are now only four standard deviations to the right of the new norm. The extreme event will still have the same intensity as before, but it won't be nearly as rare. Events that are four standard deviations to the right of the norm happen with much greater frequency that those five standard deviations to the right.

It's a sobering observation. Even though the Earth as a whole has experienced what seems to be a moderate temperature increase, its ability to generate extreme weather events has risen sharply. In climate terms, we now live in a world of tipping point dangers. Terrible events are more intense and they occur more often.

Other kinds of qualitative changes also matter. Consider the effect of a two degree increase in temperature when it's twenty-eight degrees out. For those engaged in their morning commute, the shift from twenty-eight to thirty won't be that meaningful. But if it's a shift from thirty-one to thirty-three? Especially if the streets are wet? What had started as a routine commute can swiftly become a nightmare commute.

Winter snowpacks in the Cascades and the Sierras have fallen precipitously over the past three decades, even though the global temperature increase has been relatively modest.[5] Small

---

5 - U.S. Global Change Research Program. *Global Climate Change Impacts in the United States. 2009.* https://nca2009.globalchange.gov/

temperature change; significant *climate* impact.

Once the winters in the Rocky Mountains were cold enough to wipe out pine beetles, and the pine forests of the Rockies survived nicely from one year to the next.

But now, with winters that are only modestly warmer, pine beetles haven't been killed off by the winter cold any more. When spring arrives, pine beetles begin to feed, by the millions, on the pine forests they call home. And those pine forests are now dead. Fortunately many other kinds of trees still survive, but it's startling and depressing to see pine forests standing dead, not just in Colorado, but as far north as Montana. Note the pattern: Small *temperature* change, significant *climate* impact.

If we use rules of proportionality to estimate the dangers of climate change, we will badly understate the threats ahead. It isn't rising temperatures per se that ought to be our ultimate worry; it's *climate, especially at its most intense.* Even a modest shift in the world's average temperature is capable of producing dangerous changes in regional *climate* behaviors. Over time, we will find ourselves inundated by this reality. One should already begin to fear the loss of the ice sheets on Greenland and West Antarctica. From the work scientists have already done in these locations, it seems likely that small changes in the Earth's average temperature are more than capable of producing tipping point changes in the world's major ice sheets. By all accounts, their melt speed has increase enormously in the past fifteen years.

Are these the worst of our worries? Probably not. At the extremes of a changing climate, the world is going to see terrible crop failures, and for some countries, terrible levels of starvation. We know where this leads. Climate migrations numbering in the millions. Regional wars. Intensified hostility among rival nations. And, carried to the extreme, a global political environment in which someone, somewhere, may decide it's time to throw a nuclear weapon at someone they particularly dislike.

We are headed toward a very disorienting future if we cannot get our act together and put a lid on global warming. I mentioned earlier that I had been flattened with West Nile, a disease that was completely new to me. I mentioned that my brain formed no memories of my first four days in the hospital – and that this disoriented me in ways that I had never experienced before.

Well. When it comes to the risk of being disoriented, my experience with West Nile has to rank as pure kids' stuff. A world of intensifying climate extremes will create levels of disorientation that millions of us have never seen before. A disoriented world in a time of nuclear weapons will not be nearly as safe as it ought to be.

Let's recap the cause-and-effect situation within which we – we humans – now find ourselves.

- Our technologies drive our consumption of fossil fuel.

- Our dependence on fossil fuel drives our CO_2 emissions.

- Our CO_2 emissions drive the stock of atmospheric CO_2 to higher and higher levels.

- The higher the stock of atmospheric CO_2, the higher the Earth's average temperature.

- The higher the Earth's temperature, the more intense and dangerous the Earth's climate becomes.

What an extraordinary cause-and-effect challenge! Our technologies shape our consumption, our consumption shapes our emissions, our emissions shape the atmospheric stock of CO_2, the stock of atmospheric CO_2 shapes the amount of global warming, and ongoing global warming intensifies the damage from climate change. This is a longer chain of causal reasoning than we may be accustomed to absorbing, but we cannot respond properly to this challenge until we understand its cause-and-effect properties and realize just how serious a challenge it really is.

So what more are we to learn from this?

Here's the first takeaway. Regardless of the "emissions reduction" rhetoric that has been part of this issue from the beginning, global warming is not "an emissions problem."

In the language of *flows* and *stocks*, global warming has never been caused by annual *flows* of CO_2. It has always been caused by increases to the total *stock* of CO_2. The higher the total *stock*, the more trouble we're in.

This larger threat cannot be halted, let alone reversed, until the total stock of atmospheric carbon dioxide has been safely capped.

And now to our second takeaway.

If the threat of intensifying climate change is to be checked, *all* technologies that rely on fossil fuels have to be replaced. Only by creating a clean energy future in which fossil fuels no longer have a role can we bring global warming to a complete halt.

If we practice diagnostic craftsmanship properly, this is where its logic will lead. Our reliance on fossil fuel technologies is at the root of our problem.

The Character Test

Now let's ask ourselves the Character question. Ours is a civilization of cause-and-effect systems. We have seen what happens when the world bets its future on technologies that require fossil fuels. We raise the temperature of the Earth and we imperil the global climate.

Are we willing to accept Responsibility for these causes? And for the effects they create?

A people of Character and Craftsmanship will say "Yes." We are patriots. We know our calling.

These cause-and-effect realities have put all of humanity in a box. We have been signing off on a cause-and-effect system that puts the world in peril, and we have been signing off on this system for far too long. It's time to blow the whistle on ourselves.

In Chapter 12 we will examine in more detail what our larger responsibility really looks like.

Global Warming

has never been *"an emissions reduction"* problem.

It has *always* been a fossil fuels phase-out problem.

★

Chapter Twelve

Craftsmanship
THE CLEAN ENERGY ADVENTURE

"Fossil fuels won't go away . . . until we have something better."

WERE THIS AN ERA THAT VALUED Character and Craftsmanship, it's likely that the world's political and industrial leaders would already have reached agreement on the perils of global warming and on the urgency of switching to a clean energy future.

But this is not such an era. Yes, we are handicapped in part by the realities of systemic corruption. But we are also handicapped by the diagnostic and prescriptive carelessness of so many who might already see themselves as reformers.

Prescriptive Craftsmanship

What if our thought leaders on this issue had been up to the challenge? If our scientific and environmental leaders had been more rigorous and thoughtful, what sort of path forward would they have recommended?

First of all, they'd have mastered the challenges of diagnostic craftsmanship. They would have taught us to understand the cause-and-effect situation in which we find ourselves.

And, second, they would have used that logic to guide our vision of the journey ahead. In broad terms, here's the solution framework they would have placed before us, even in the 1970s:

- *Unchecked climate change will cause far more damage than the world can afford. Climate change has to be contained (and then reversed).*

- *For climate change to be contained, global warming must first be halted.*

- *For global warming to be halted, the stock of atmospheric CO_2 has to stop growing.*

- *For the stock of atmospheric CO_2 to stop growing, emissions of CO_2 from fossil fuels must first be halted.*

- *For CO_2 emissions from fossil fuels to be halted, the consumption of fossil fuels must be halted.*

- *For the consumption of fossil fuels to be halted, all technologies that require fossil fuels need to be replaced with new and climate-safe alternatives.*

- *The threats ahead are severe and growing. We are in a race against time. It's important to America and to all humanity that we win the race to a clean energy future.*

A tough message, yes? But it brings our challenge into focus, it gets us on target. It is how we step up to the challenges of Character and Craftsmanship.

Think of the scenario ahead as a handyman's adventure. We switch from one energy system in which fuel was something we always had to buy, to a new energy system where much of its fuel cost is essentially zero. Sunshine is free. Wind is free. Wave energy is free. Yes, we have to spend capital dollars to capture the world's free energy, but we don't have to pay for the energy itself.

A clean energy future is a feasible goal – difficult, but feasible, and much the best answer for all humanity in the decades and centuries ahead.

Here in America, if we do our very best, we might succeed by 2050. For the world as a whole – if everyone does his or her best

– the transition to a clean energy future might require a couple decades beyond that.

Let's think of it this way. There's enormous power to the American mass market, both on the buying side and on the producing side. Harness that power on behalf of tomorrow's clean energy future and we will accelerate not only our own transition, but also the world's transition. Technologies that we perfect, and then produce affordably, become everyone's solution.

The faster we move our own industries down the clean energy cost curve, the more we'll stimulate faster adoption rates throughout the world. The faster we get smart, the faster we get cheap, and the faster we get cheap, the faster our worldwide sprint to the finish line.

Conversely, if we forget that America is an extraordinary nation, if we choose to be heel-dragging followers instead of highly-motivated leaders, the more fossil fuel consumption of which we and others will be guilty. The more growth we'll see in the atmosphere's CO_2 overload. The more global warming the Earth will suffer. And the more deadly the process of climate change will become.

A world of failing crops will be a world of intensifying wars, climate refugees, and incensed terrorists. A world of simmering wars everywhere is a world that could find itself on the edge of using nuclear weapons. Procrastinating in the face of our global warming challenge could well metastasize into a devastating strategic error.

In the journey ahead, we begin with two major factors working in our favor. On any given day, America's end users consume about 57 terawatt-hours worth of energy. And, on any given day, America receives about 50,000 terawatt-hours worth of sunshine. If we capture but a thousandth of all the solar energy that's available to us, we'll have quite enough to power America's entire economy.

Beyond that, America's wind potential is also up to the challenge. Were we to deploy wind turbines to our nation's fullest capacity, we'd end up with 12 terawatts of wind capacity.[1] Assume, conservatively, that all these turbines, together, average five hours of output every day. That works out to 60 terawatt-hours of energy generated every day – slightly more than our entire economy now consumes.

Combine those two sources. Sunshine, captured by solar panels, and Wind, captured by wind turbines. America's potential to generate renewable energy is far more extensive than we will ever need.

But this isn't just a story of big numbers and big infrastructure. What we face here is also a story of individuals and families, a story of homes and apartments and cars; a story about us and the gadgets by which we power our lives.

My wife and I have taken an important step forward. We built our home in 1994; in 2015, we took our home off fossil fuels. Completely. No more natural gas. No more coal-fired electricity.

How did we do this? Mostly by doing things that come naturally to any homeowner. Our hot water heaters were electric from the start. No natural gas there. We replaced our gas stove with an electric stove more than ten years ago, mostly for health reasons. In the spring of 2015, as the gas furnace in our basement began to falter, we learned that it would be simple to swap it out for a geothermal heat pump. Now everything in the home runs on electricity; nothing runs on natural gas.

And where do we get our electricity? From the BGE grid, of course. Our electricity dollars, though, are dedicated to the purchase of wind-generated electricity. Not a penny of what we

------

1 - Downloaded Excel File: wind_potential_80m_120m_140m_35percent.xlsx, from AWS Truepower study for the National Renewable Energy Lab. 12 TW maximum wind capacity calculation based on each state's highest potential wind rating. Alaska omitted.

spend for electricity ends up in the pockets of coal or natural gas companies.

And the wind-generated electricity is affordable. We are part of a group-purchasing program that keeps our electricity costs down. Our cost per kilowatt-hour is only a fraction of a cent higher than it would be if we were still using electricity generated from fossil fuels – on a monthly basis, half the cost of a movie ticket.

It's an attractive energy package. Clean energy electricity, clean energy hot water heaters, clean energy cooking, clean energy heating and air conditioning. The energy portfolio that powers our home is part of the solution. And with the geothermal heat pump, we find our annual utility bill has fallen by several hundred dollars.

Now we're waiting for Tesla to produce an electric car with the range we want and at a price we can afford. When that day comes, we'll buy a Tesla and use our 2004 Prius as our trade-in. After a few more years, we'll trade in our 2011 Prius for another Tesla.

Multiply what we have done by a hundred million homes or so. As a nation, we dig ourselves out of our dirty energy hole the same way we dug ourselves in – one consumer purchase at a time, one homeowner purchase at a time, one vehicle purchase at a time, one electricity contract at a time. And what holds for homeowners like us also holds for our nation and all nations, everywhere – we make the journey to our clean energy future one capital purchase at a time, one consumer purchase at a time.

Prescriptive Thinking on a National Scale

There is a larger story to be told about the path to a clean energy future, but hardly anyone tells it properly.

The first thing to know is that it's not just a story about electricity (even if some environmentalists act as though it is). Yes, it's good to see so much wind power being installed. Yes, it's good to see coal plants closing. Yes, it's interesting to read about something as exotic as the Ivanpah generating plant in Southern California, with its vast array of mirrors and its high temperature solar heating tower.

The larger story is the systemic story. Our journey to a clean energy future is simultaneously a journey of little guys and a journey of systemic transformation. To come to grips with the systemic character of this transformation, it's essential that we begin by taking a holistic view of this nation's entire energy system.

You might think of this as something too complex to be understood. Here I hope to show you that America's energy system – while complex – is something we can grasp if we examine its parts patiently and figure out how they fit together.

Not simple. But within reach. Here I offer a Sources & Uses Chart. The text that follows will take you through the logic and the rough magnitudes.

Here's the insight I hope you will get. It won't be enough for our reformers to focus their attention solely on climate-safe energy *Source* technologies. It's just as essential to focus on all our economy's *Use* technologies, and ensure that all of them have escaped from their fossil fuel beginnings.

By *Source Technologies*, I mean wind and solar and hydropower and nuclear and biofuels and others as well.

By *Use Technologies*, I mean the technologies that heat our Buildings, that power our Industries, and that propel our Transportation system.

We need both revolutions – an Energy *Sources* Revolution, and an Energy *Uses* Revolution – if we are to halt our reliance on fossil fuels.

Or, to make the same point more colloquially, we need a future that will be known both for its clean energy *power* and for its clean energy *gadgets*.

Fig. 12.1	SOURCES AND USES CHART							
	U.S. Energy in Terawatt Hours/Day (2015) (Chart contains rounding errors.)							
SOURCES / USES	Electricity Generation	Residential Uses	Commercial Uses	Industrial Uses	Transportation (Gasoline)	Transportation (Diesel)	Transportation (Jet Aviation)	SOURCE TOTALS
FOSSIL FUEL								
Coal	3.71	0.00	0.04	1.12				4.88
Petroleum	0.07	0.79	0.45	6.59	13.35	5.28	2.57	29.11
Natural Gas	3.64	3.80	2.64	7.48				17.55
ELECTRICITY								
Nuclear	2.18							2.18
Hydro	0.68							0.68
Wind	0.52							0.52
Biomass-Wood	0.04			0.07				0.12
Geothermal-E	0.05							0.05
Biomass-Waste	0.05							0.05
Solar	0.07	0.23	0.02					0.31
LIQUID FUEL								
Ethanol					0.32			0.32
Biodiesel						0.15		0.15
HEAT								
Biomass-Wood		0.35	0.06	1.04				1.44
Geothermal-H		0.03	0.02	0.00				0.05
LOSSES	- 0.55							- 0.55
NET ELECTRICITY	10.47	3.83	3.72	2.90	0.02			
		Resid'l	Comm'l	Indust'l	Tran: Gas	Tran: Diesel	Tran: Jet	
USE TOTALS		9.03	6.95	19.19	13.69	5.44	2.57	56.87

Figure 12.1 Energy Information Administration. Monthly Energy Review for any time period post-2014. Author's calculations.

This means that our *Sources and Uses Chart* can also be understood as a *Power Sources and Gadgets Chart*.

In yesterday's America, we ran our economy with dirty energy power and dirty energy gadgets. In tomorrow's economy, we will run our economy with clean energy *power* and clean energy gadgets.

Now, back to the table. Using data extracted from the U.S. Government's Monthly Energy Review, I have built Figure 12.1 to give the careful reader a handle on the interaction between energy *sources* and energy *uses*.

And, because we are moving away from heat energy (measured in British Thermal Units) and toward electric energy (measured in watt-hours), my chart converts the BTU tables of yesterday into the watt-hour standard of tomorrow.

Or, in this case, not watt-hours per day but Terawatt-Hours per Day, for all Sources and for all Uses. In today's era of computers, we have already been trained to think in terms of kilobytes, megabytes, gigabytes, and even terabytes. Wrapping our minds around kilowatt-hours, megawatt-hours, gigawatt-hours, and terawatt-hours shouldn't be that much of a stretch.

As you will learn from this table, the American economy produced, and consumed, 56.87 terawatt-hours/day of energy in 2015.

Down the left side, the table lists the nation's chief energy *Sources* – Fossil Fuels, Electricity, Liquid Fuels, and Heat. On the right side of the table, running down, you will see totals for each Source. Coal provided 4.88 TWH/Day worth of source energy, petroleum provided 29.11, and so on. The Grand Total for all Sources, 56.87 TWH/Day, is at the bottom.

Across the top, the table lists the nation's chief energy *Uses* – starting with Electricity Generation, then Residential Uses, Commercial Uses, Industrial Uses, Transportation (Gasoline), Transportation (Diesel), and Transportation (Jet & Aviation Fuel).

Let's begin with the *Electricity Generation* column. Electricity Generation begins as a user of energy, and then turns around and becomes a source of energy. Its dual identity gives it a special place here.

Work your way down this column and you'll see all the different methods our nation has for producing electricity. We burn coal and we burn natural gas, and from those two fuels we derive about sixty-seven percent of our electricity. We operate nuclear power plants and they give us about twenty percent of the nation's electricity. Hydroelectric power accounts for six percent, wind power for five percent, and smaller categories for the remainder.

Continue down the electricity column. "Line Losses" shrink the total by a little more than half a terawatt-hour/day, leaving 10.47 TWH/Day of Net Electricity.

Then, if you like, trace your finger across this row to see who actually consumes the nation's electricity. Residential Users consume 3.83 TWH/Day. Commercial Users consume 3.72 TWH/Day. And so on.

Let's go back to the top and pick up the rest of the nation's *Uses.* You will see six more columns – Residential Uses, Commercial Uses, Industrial Uses, Transportation (Gasoline), Transportation (Diesel), and Transportation (Jet, Aviation).

Now go all the way to the bottom row, and read across. In Terawatt-Hours/Day, you will learn how much energy each of these Uses required in 2015.

Residential:	9.03 TWH/Day
Commercial:	6.95
Industrial:	19.19
Transportation (Gasoline):	13.69
Transportation (Diesel):	5.44
Transportation (Jet, Aviation):	2.57

The Big Picture is this. Ninety percent of America's total energy still comes from fossil fuels. *Ninety percent.* If global warming is to be halted, with America doing its part, fossil fuels as a source of power have to drop all the way from ninety percent to zero. Other forms of energy have to rise all the way from ten percent to a hundred percent.

This may not be something we *want* to do. In a way, nobody wants to do this. But we *have* to do it.

The tragedy of this challenge is that America's thought leaders haven't stepped up. Supposedly it's enough that the U.S. sent negotiators to Paris. Supposedly it's enough to have demonstrations on behalf of less CO_2 in the atmosphere. Supposedly it's enough to call on Stanford and Harvard and hundreds of others to rid their portfolios of fossil fuel stocks. Supposedly it's enough to call for "keeping fossil fuels in the ground." Supposedly it's enough to call for a tax on carbon fuels with the proceeds to be rebated back to the public.

There's a lot of spirited protest under way, no doubt about it. But does any of it really have the gravitas our times demand? As mentioned before, our instincts teach us to be incremental thinkers. But global warming cannot be halted with incremental responses. We are up against a transformational challenge, and it's time for us to muster a transformational response.

On this issue, especially, more than on any other, Prescriptive Craftsmanship absolutely *requires* transformational thinking.

America's reliance on fossil fuels has to end. Completely. And so too for the world. Everyone's reliance on fossil fuels has to be phased out. Completely. It's the only way to contain the threat we face.

If we are to bring global warming to a complete halt, as we must, all players will have to sign on for the transformational journey ahead.

Residential energy use? We shall have to phase out fossil fuels in our homes and apartments. A hundred million of them, perhaps. Not easy. But also a handyman's opportunity.

Commercial energy use? Same requirement.

Industrial energy use? Every piece of industrial equipment that requires fossil fuels has to be replaced with new equipment that doesn't. Not just here, in America, but everywhere. Every factory from which we Americans buy our goods – at home and across the globe – needs to be off fossil fuels, completely, by mid-century.

Vehicles powered by gasoline? Every type of vehicle that runs on gasoline today needs to be equipped with something different tomorrow. For some applications, battery storage and electric motors and ubiquitous charging stations will do the trick. In other applications, ammonia or ethanol or methanol or biodiesel fuels or even hydrogen will fuel the technologies of tomorrow.

Vehicles powered by diesel fuels? Ocean freighters will always need liquid fuel of some kind. (In a world of pirates and terrorists, nuclear energy will never be a safe answer for ocean freighters.)

Can tomorrow's eighteen-wheelers be powered with batteries and electric motors? Elon Musk probably thinks so, and he might be right. But there may be a better answer. It will be interesting to see what sort of answer Cummins develops!

Aircraft powered by aviation fuel or jet fuel? Stanford's Mark Jacobson thinks that frozen hydrogen will prove to be aviation's best choice. According to Jacobson, hydrogen fuel in its frozen state will be slightly bulkier than jet fuel but it won't weigh as much, and it will deliver roughly the same amount of power as today's aviation fuels. Will tomorrow's jet aircraft be powered by frozen hydrogen? Or by some other alternative to the petroleum fuels of today? Boeing and Airbus cannot stay with fossil fuels; they will have to find climate-safe alternatives.

On the SOURCES side of the equation, several more sets of daunting challenges will require our very best.

Odds are the nation will require three or four times as much electricity as it generates today – and all of it will have to from clean power sources.

Liquid fuels will be essential, but two daunting constraints have to be coped with. There's almost surely not enough cropland – globally – to feed humanity's potential appetite for liquid fuels. When croplands for biodiesel fuels and ethanol fuels max out, as they surely will, odds are that ammonia and hydrogen will become part of tomorrow's liquid fuel solution.

And then there's the matter of direct heat, now obtained from burning fossil fuels and biomass. What's the future demand for direct heat likely to be, and what's likely to be the best set of sources for direct heat?

The proper way to go at this is to affirm our transformational objectives. All our energy sources will be clean; all our energy uses will be clean; and we'll have the transformation wholly completed by 2060.

And then I would add Phase-Out Deadlines, Acts of Congress that set phase-out deadlines for vehicle types, for industrial equipment, and for buildings. No more gasoline vehicles sold after 2035. No more gasoline filling stations in operation after 2050. No more natural gas furnaces or heating oil furnaces in new buildings after 2025. And so on, across the entire spectrum.

It's a journey of small steps, and also a journey of complete liberation. We adopt tomorrow's new energy system the same way we adopted yesterday's fossil fuel energy system – one capital purchase at a time, one consumer purchase at a time.

Two more challenges require our focused attention.

Soft Landing Plans. How is the nation to look after those communities whose livelihoods now depend on fossil fuels? Can they become manufacturing centers for clean energy technologies? We have gone through this before with communities that lost their military bases. What did we learn from the Base Realignment and Closure process (BRAC) that will help with tomorrow's transitions? The better we are at helping these communities transition gently to the economy of tomorrow, the easier it will be to keep the entire nation moving forward toward a future without fossil fuels.

CO₂ Extraction. The nations of the world won't meet their aspirational deadlines for phasing out fossil fuels – that's already clear. We should try to get mostly done by 2050 and all done by 2060, but even if we meet those targets, we will find that we have badly overshot our margin of error. The atmosphere will have accumulated much more CO_2 than we can safely accept.

Rising temperatures, dangerous climate changes, and melting ice sheets will be much further along by 2050 and 2060 than the world can afford. Today's complacency will have long since given way to a global sense of climate panic.

Future generations will be desperate to pull carbon dioxide out of the atmosphere.

How are we to think about this challenge? Let's start by acknowledging its raw size. My rough calculations suggest an eventual carbon overload of one quadrillion pounds, divided between the atmosphere and the oceans.

In other words, if we could pull one quadrillion pounds of carbon out of the air and the oceans and hide it someplace, we'd get the world's atmosphere back to 280 Parts Per Million.

Where would we hide it? Is there any chance of us extracting CO_2 from the atmosphere, splitting the carbon away from the oxygen, and jamming all that carbon back into the ground? Into all the coal mines, oil wells, and natural gas wells that were its original sources? Obviously not. We'll have to find a better approach.

Many possibilities will be tested. Just for the sake of argument, let's assume that photosynthesis turns out to be our best hope. Let's assume that we use photosynthesis to coax CO_2 out of the atmosphere, capture the carbon, and then induce all these enriched root systems to hold the trapped carbon indefinitely.

Shall we put some numbers to this in order to appreciate just how daunting a task this will become?

Let's postulate fourteen million square miles of land being suitable for this task. That's about a quarter of the land area of the Earth (not counting Antarctica).

And let's imagine ourselves managing all this land – all this farm land, all this pasture land – with advanced land management techniques. On all this land, all fourteen million square miles of it, we boost soil carbon by three pounds per square foot. That's right. Three pounds of extra carbon, per square *foot*, across fourteen million square *miles* of land.

Do that, and we will have pulled one quadrillion pounds of carbon out of the air and trapped it permanently in the soil.

How would farmers and pasture managers be induced to adjust their land management methods toward this goal? I don't know. Certainly they'll deserve to be paid.

How long would it take to recapture most of the atmosphere's excess carbon? Quite a long time, I should think. All the more reason to set the wheels in motion sooner rather than later.

How Might We Celebrate Our Success?

Suppose it's 2045 and we have reached the point where the last gasoline-powered automobiles are about to be pulled from service in the United States. How might we mark the moment?

I propose a raffle. The last group of drivers to own gasoline-powered cars are invited to enter the raffle. Or, better yet, two raffles, one for men and one for women.

Two drawings are held. The winning man and the winning woman are invited to drive their cars in victory laps at the Daytona 500 and the Indianapolis 500.

Then, once they've taken their victory laps, the Henry Ford Museum in Dearborn, Michigan, buys their cars and puts them on display. Think of it. The last two gasoline powered cars in America, alongside the museum's Newcomen Steam Engine. Bookends to the Era of Fossil Fuels.

And, as another bow to sentiment, perhaps the ancient Maryland steam engine that now makes a weekly run between Frostburg and Cumberland should be kept in service till it gives out.

We will have mixed feelings in saying "Good-bye" to the era of fossil fuels. We enjoyed the cars, the trains, the airplanes, the motorcycles. And we'll still have cars, and trains, and airplanes, and motorcycles, but when we see it all running on batteries and electric motors and who knows what else, I'm sure we'll feel pangs of regret.

When the time comes to say Good-Bye, let's say a proper Good-Bye. We loved all the machines that made the Era of Fossil Fuels what it was. And even though we have to leave that era forever behind, our hearts won't let us forget. When the time comes, let's send it off in style!

What Does This Teach Us About Ourselves?

The journey I have sketched in this chapter is a transformational journey. Yes, it will have to be pursued with incremental steps, to be sure, but it's still a transformational journey.

Imagining and visualizing this sort of journey won't come easily. Our instincts teach us to be gradualists. We deal with what's in front of us and we make gradual adjustments.

Transformational thinking so often feels like a sideline. Steve Jobs was a transformational thinker, from inside Apple. Elon Musk is a transformational thinker. Good for them. As for the rest of us, well, we imagine that gradualism is all we shall ever need.

Even the nation's largest environmental groups haven't been up to the challenge of interpreting what lies ahead in transformational terms. They haven't acted with a strong enough sense of Character. They have lacked diagnostic craftsmanship. And they certainly didn't have enough prescriptive craftsmanship to show the rest of us what the path forward would actually look like.

They wouldn't name the problem – atmospheric CO_2 has to be capped.

They wouldn't name the transformation that has to take place. All technologies that require fossil fuels have to be replaced with new technologies that don't require fossil fuels.

They wouldn't set hard deadlines. They wouldn't insist on phase-out plans for each set of technologies that have to be replaced.

They blew their responsibility. They should have described history's demands – let go of fossil fuels. Develop safe and effective alternatives. Instead they gave us soundbites – "emission reduction" soundbites – that mischaracterized the problem and pointed everyone in the wrong direction.

Why? Because, like the rest of us, they weren't instinctively equipped to visualize transformational options *even in those situations where transformational change is the only safe answer.*

Let's learn from this. Sometimes the *only* way to get ourselves truly unstuck is to choose the transformational option.

It should *never* be against the rules to visualize transformational options for handling major problems. Transformational options won't always be necessary, but they should never be taken off the table before the hard work of analyzing the problem has even begun.

The Politics of Character and Craftsmanship will call for a receptive spirit toward all sorts of possible solutions. If our society's recognized thought leaders had been more foresighted on all this, humanity could have gotten a stronger head start.

If we capture but a **thousandth** of the solar energy available to us, we can power our *entire* economy.

Getting America **UnStuck**
The Politics of **Character** & **Craftsmanship**

americaunstuck.com

★

Chapter Thirteen

Craftsmanship

THE SUSTAINABLITY CHALLENGE

"Preparing to sing God's praises for the next ten thousand years."

THE ENERGY CHALLENGE, DIFFICULT AS IT IS, gives us just a hint of what it means to coexist responsibly with Mother Nature here on Planet Earth. Let's take Character and Craftsmanship as our standards and ask an even larger and harder question: How are we to live responsibly on the Earth for all generations to come? We humans? We Americans?

This is the ultimate test of our character, as inheritors of a human civilization, as inheritors of Nature's kingdoms. Can we create a healthy civilization for ourselves, for all generations to come? Can we do it in a way that protects Nature's well-being, also for all generations to come?

If we insist on approaching this challenge from within an ethos of systemic corruption, the answer will be "No." Humanity cannot build a lasting civilization from within the bad habits of systemic corruption. Corruption at a vast scale will undermine both Nature's well-being and also humanity's well-being.

Just look at what's already gone wrong. The Top One Percent is presently out of control. It extorts too much wealth from the weak. It protects the dirty reign of the Fossil Fuel Sector. It protects the corrupt reign of a cartel-like medical sector. It promotes systemic corruption in politics and in the media.

So long as the dark forces of systemic corruption hold the upper hand, our quest for a sustainable future will inevitably be cut short.

But hold. The forces of systemic corruption remain in control only at our sufferance. We can change that by saying "No" to systemic corruption in all its forms, and by saying "Yes" to Character and Craftsmanship as our guiding ethos going forward. It's time to do this not just as Americans, but as partners with people of integrity all across the globe.

Let's suppose that we have taken this on and that we have gained the upper hand. The forces of systemic corruption have for the most part been shut down.

How, in tomorrow's reformed world, are we to visualize humanity's long-run partnership with Nature? (As you will sense, this is the question our spirit of Prescriptive Craftsmanship will expect us to ask.)

The headlines ought to be clear. We will want human societies everywhere to be societies of prosperity and well-being. And we will want Nature's kingdoms to be respected and vigorous. Nature's well-being supports our well-being; our well-being supports Nature's well-being.

But that won't be quite enough.

From within an ethos of Prescriptive Craftsmanship, we will want to go further. There are a few things one can say, even now, about the disciplines by which human societies will need to operate over the centuries and millennia to come.

Let's start with what we already know about ourselves, as a tribal species that's been around quite a long time.

There are five constants to human existence that we have to take into account:

- We are a species that always has babies.
  We always have been, we always will be.

- We are a species that always occupies land. We always have been, we always will be.

- We are a species that always acquires resources – for tools, for clothing, for food, and for much else. We always have been, we always will be.

- We are a species that produces and consumes goods. Always have been, always will be.

- And we are a species that generates waste. Always have been, always will be.

These core realities are a given. They name traits that will always be with us, traits that humanity will have to manage responsibly if it is to live responsibly on Planet Earth.

A spirit of responsible management instinctively applies a matched set of disciplines, rules to honor and live within if we humans are to assure ourselves of a lasting and healthy future.

Ending Our Addiction to Growth

In our hearts, I think we already know what the challenge is. We haven't broken our addiction to endless growth. We have large appetites and our appetites continue to expand. More and more babies. More and more land occupied. More and more resources extracted and consumed. More production, and still more. More consumption, and still more. More and more waste to throw away.

At the same time, even as we indulge our appetites, we also know that our planet is finite. Yes, we are in the habit of wanting more. And more, and still more. But our planet has limits. Take too much, and we wear out the planet on which we live.

How are we to shape a future for ourselves that works well on both fronts? How are we to have a future in which Nature thrives, and humanity as well, at the same time?

What an interesting test of our capacity for Character! Of our capacity for Prescriptive Craftsmanship!!

Are we up to it? Can we find a way of reshaping our own habits so that we humans strike a proper balance with Nature, for all generations?

Yes, as with the story of the ashes and the white sheets, this is a test of our self-restraint, of our responsibility, of our Character. Beyond that, it will be a test of our capacities for diagnostic and prescriptive craftsmanship.

Are we up to it? The answer might be "No." The Catholic Church couldn't stop itself from letting its priests abuse its children. Perhaps we won't have the guts to stop ourselves from destroying Nature's well-being.

On the other hand, the answer might be "Yes." Perhaps we will teach ourselves to show the Character and the Craftsmanship that's needed.

It is up to us. Can we raise future generations to have the same kind of self-discipline our parents wanted us to have?

Here's what we will have to teach ourselves about the disciplines that Mother Nature demands of us. Think five guiding principles. Think the "Five Zeroes of Sustainability."

1. **Zero Net Increase in Population;**
2. **Zero Net Loss of Habitat;**
3. **Zero Net Loss of Resources;**
4. **Zero Cumulative Pollution;**
5. **Zero Cumulative Waste.**

Let's consider each of these as a guiding scenario. And let's test each of these with a pair of "What Ifs."

- What if we stabilize our population?
  What if we don't?

- What if we protect habitat successfully, all across the planet? What if we don't?

- What if we conserve and recycle the world's resources? What if we don't?

- What if we take zero cumulative pollution as our standard? What if we don't?

- What if we take zero cumulative waste as our standard? What if we don't?

In the past two chapters, I argued the case for zero cumulative pollution of the atmosphere as a guiding standard, as an imperative within which we are to shape tomorrow's portfolio of clean energy technologies. And I have argued the case for Transformational Craftsmanship, as the only approach to humanity's energy future that can bring us to safe harbor.

Now expand this spirit of craftsmanship to encompass all five of the sustainability disciplines listed above. Use diagnostic craftsmanship to assess the challenges we face. Use prescriptive craftsmanship to find the wisest possible solutions.

Character and Craftsmanship can lead us toward a prosperous and sustainable future. Manage ourselves well, and all humanity can enjoy widespread prosperity. Manage ourselves well, and the partnership between Nature and Humanity can last for thousands and even millions of years.

Let's put a little more detail behind each of these Five Zeroes.

1. Zero Net Increase In Population. The first discipline in living sustainably for all generations is for humanity to limit its birth rate. As humanity's overall death rate continues its decline, our overall birth rate will need to decline as well. We will live in balance with the Earth by voluntarily limiting our numbers.

The world has already seen significant successes on this front. Girls who go to school choose smaller families. Young women who have been given reproductive counseling choose smaller families. The liberation of girls and women is one of the keys to long-run population stability. But we haven't gone all the way. There's more to do.

2. Zero Net Loss Of Habitat. The second discipline of living sustainably for all generations will be built on a respect for Nature, for its vitality and perpetual health. Nature's realm is the realm of natural habitats. The Creator didn't entrust humans with stewardship of the Earth so that we would become marauders, plunderers, rapists, exterminators, and destroyers. The Creator gave us the Earth as a blessing, and charged us with being its careful stewards.

If we are wise, we will see ourselves as being in the Creator's debt, and we will respect the responsibilities we have been given.

In other words, we are to be held responsible – by the Creator and by our own good Character - for respecting Nature's many habitats and for living in balance with Nature from one generation to the next, to the next, and to the next. We are entrusted with responsibility for the Earth's lasting well-being. As this nation's indigenous peoples like to remind us, "We borrow the Earth from our descendants."

3. Zero Net Loss Of Resources. As our third discipline, we acknowledge finite limits to Nature's resources; we vow to respect those limits so that Nature's bounty will be with us from everlasting to everlasting.

Here's one of the tests that we will face. Modern industrial agriculture depends on regular inputs of phosphorus, obtained from the world's phosphorus mines. These supplies are finite; the time will come when today's mines have been played out.

To be sure, there will be other phosphorus deposits, not quite as good, that will take their place. And then others. But note the gamble that's built into this way of doing business. Agricultural productivity – in today's business model – is closely tied to a wasting resource. No one should think of this as a stable arrangement, not one that can endure until the end of time.

Peasant agriculture operated differently. A family's outhouse was also its fertilizer collection point, its fertilizer storehouse. Waste urine and waste feces were collected and worked back into the soil, in rituals of enrichment that reaffirmed the endless cycles of nature.

These lessons remind us that the business models on which our civilization has been built need to be tested. Do they meet the Third Zero Test? Do they fulfill the standard, "Zero Net Loss of Resources"?

Where we find business models that fail the test, we will need to apply the rules of Character and Craftsmanship. What will it take to create business models that meet this larger test?

This same question arises in the world of e-waste. So many rare and precious metals go into the manufacture of a modern computer. What happens to all those precious metals when the computer wears out? In many parts of the world, e-waste simply gets dumped into landfill, to be picked over by children in poorer parts of the world. Yes, they earn a few pennies by retrieving the waste, but in the process they expose themselves to poisonous toxins. It's a terrible business model.

There is a working solution, and the Europeans, at least, are onto it. Umicore is a Belgian company with a long history of smelting precious metals. Its roots lie in Belgium's rape of the Belgian Congo, but today's Umicore has broken with that past. Now all of Europe's e-waste is gathered and delivered to Umicore. The company smelts it down and converts it back into its original constituents. Yesterday's e-waste becomes today's fresh ore. The key to its business model is to be found in the organized collection system by which European e-waste is recaptured and delivered to Umicore.

Here in the U.S., we have not organized ourselves well enough, yet, to be able to match Umicore's performance. But that could change. There is a way to recapture all the precious metals that play vital roles in electronics, and to re-use them again and again and again. Zero Net Loss of Resources is an essential standard for how human civilization needs to operate over the long run; it is also an achievable standard.

4. Zero Cumulative Pollution. Imagine a world in which thousands of companies engage in business practices that leave behind trails of permanent pollution – some grossly obvious and others very nearly invisible. In such a world, harmful compounds accumulate in the environment, creating toxic habitats, causing genetic damage to the young of countless species, poisoning the food chain, and causing sickness and even death in any number of visible and invisible ways.

Some of those untested compounds will creep into the breast milk of nursing mothers; some will creep into the foods we eat; some will become part of the air we breathe, some will damage the developing brains of young children.

Faulty business models yield damaging outcomes. Are we okay with that?

There will be those who will rationalize such business practices as the legitimate working of the Free Market. Give every industry a license to pollute and what will happen? We'll see Race to The Bottom Industrialism. Instead of Character, and a loyalty to standards of decency, we will have Morality Play rationalizations. "Sine I create jobs, I am not to be held responsible for the trails of poison I leave in my wake."

Zero cumulative pollution is the business standard by which human society protects the well-being of the Earth and all its inhabitants.

5. Zero Cumulative Waste. The fifth discipline of lasting Sustainability warns us against the sin of treating the Earth as a giant waste dump. In major metropolitan areas, this is already a pressing issue. Here in a semi-urban, semi-rural Anne Arundel County, those in charge of the county dump have said they expect to run out of landfill capacity within the fairly near future.

And this is a county with a strong recycling program. Waste Management built what's called a "single waste stream" recycling plant in our county some years ago, capable of separating paper and cardboard and aluminum cans and plastic bottles and on and on. If I leave a bag of newspaper by the curb on Wednesday evening, four weeks later that same newsprint will have been cleaned of its ink, remade into new rolls of newsprint, and delivered to subscribers as fresh newspapers. Single waste stream recycling is probably as strong in Anne Arundel County as it is anywhere in the country, and still Anne Arundel County faces the challenge of where to put its waste when the current dump finally runs out of room.

There's much more to the principle of Zero Cumulative Waste than what you and I will see as consumers. Extraction waste and production waste are far more challenging. Traditional mining is notorious for scarring the landscape and leaving behind toxic mine tailings.

All sorts of waste streams will need to be examined as we do our best to live up to this standard. Think about ships at sea, a world not just of giant freighter companies but of rogue operators as well. Who knows what sort of filth those operators pitch into the world's oceans, on the general theory that unseen misdeeds will never be detected, let alone punished?

We are still a people that pitch cigarette butts out our car windows as we're waiting at red lights, little caring about the litter we leave behind. From my cab driving days, I remember a colleague who sometimes cheated on his wife, theorizing that a bit of cheating would be okay as long as she didn't find out. "What the eye can't see, the heart can't grieve," he would tell himself. Disappointing . . . and yet isn't that the *modus operandi* of many a ship's crew? "We won't be held accountable for what other people can't see us do."

To live within the discipline of "Zero cumulative waste," we will do well to learn from the recommendations offered by William McDonough and Michael Braungart in *Cradle to Cradle*.[1] Treat everything in yesterday's waste stream as a mixture of organic nutrients and technical nutrients; treat everything in tomorrow's input stream for manufacturing in the same way, as a mixture of organic and technical nutrients. With this framework as a guiding norm, we can find our way toward business models in which the world's waste streams of yesterday also become the world's production input streams of tomorrow.

One won't always have to see waste as a negative; future generations will learn to see today's waste streams and tomorrow's input streams as two parts of the same larger process. Recapture everything – organic nutrients and technical nutrients alike. Feed both sets of nutrients into the next round of production.

The long run goal is to treat *all* of today's waste as tomorrow's inputs. The discipline of zero cumulative waste turns the back end of one ancient behavior – "generating waste" – into the front end of another ancient behavior – "acquiring resources."

Character and Sustainability

These five disciplines don't do away with humanity's basic traits. We will continue to have babies, to occupy land, to acquire resources, to produce and consume goods, and to dispose of waste.

---

1 - William McDonough, Michael Braungart. *Cradle to Cradle: Remaking the Way We Make Things.* North Point Press. 2002.

But these disciplines can help us alter the methods and the rates by which we do what we have always done. Follow them carefully and human civilization will succeed at meeting its grandest challenge – that of binding together traditions of Sustainability with the traditions of Prosperity. We will be honorable partners for Nature and Nature will support an abundant Prosperity for us.

If your traditions incline you to think of Sustainability in Biblical terms, let's link the disciplines of Sustainability with the larger dream of a Promised Land. By securing Prosperity within a framework of Sustainability, we fulfill our obligations to the Creator, and we benefit from the Blessings the Creator has helped us protect.

The Promised Land is not for the arrogant; it is for the humble, for those of good character. The Promised Land is for civilizations that possess a spirit of restraint and responsibility. We can be that civilization, and we will be, once we master the Five Disciplines of Sustainability.

The last verse of *Amazing Grace* – with a small tweak – celebrates our brighter future:

> *"When we've been here ten thousand years,*
> *"Bright shining as the sun,*
> *"We've no less days to sing God's praise,*
> *"Than when we'd first begun."*

★

If we humans teach ourselves
to live within the
Five Zeroes of Sustainability,
nature will thrive and humans
will thrive for countless
thousands of years
to come.

Getting America **UnStuck**
The Politics of **Character** & **Craftsmanship**

americaunstuck.com

Chapter Fourteen

Craftsmanship
THE CLEAN POLITICS CHALLENGE

"Why do we permit politicians to pick the voters they want?"

IS A WEALTHY DEMOCRACY CONDEMNED TO LIVE in a state of permanent political corruption? Here in America, the current answer would seem to be "Yes." The more corrupt our economy becomes, the more its wealth accumulates in the hands of those at the very top. As a natural corollary, the more expensive the nation's elections become, the more corrupt the nation's politicians seem to become.

That, at least, is the mess we seem to have created for ourselves. A cause-and-effect spiral has taken hold. Corrupt laws encourage corrupt business behavior; corrupt business behaviors accelerate the enrichment of those at the top; intensified wealth at the top facilitates major spending on political campaigns; and the dependence on large donors intensifies the corruptibility of elected officials.

Now that so many voters are brand-conscious – "I vote only for conservatives" or "I vote only for liberals" – there's almost nothing to interrupt the cycle. For the conservative voter, a corrupted conservative will almost always seems better than an honest liberal; for the liberal voter, a corrupted liberal will almost always seems better than an honest conservative.

And for the moment, it doesn't seem to be in anyone's interest to campaign for something better.

There was a time when elected officials in both parties made appeals to the national interest. Conservatives and liberals both saluted the national interest as the proper way to legitimize themselves with their constituents.

There was a time when the system hadn't quite sold its soul. Now it has. Wall Street crashed the entire economy in 2008, putting millions out of work; neither party sent anyone from Wall Street to jail. No sin is too gross to rattle the cozy alliances at the top.

"Government of the people, by the people, and for the people" is not how today's national parties actually function.

"Government *of* the bottom ninety, *by* the top ten, and *for* the top one," seems to have become the tacit norm for both parties. The Republicans, naturally enough, are the Party of the Top One Percent – though they sometimes pretend not to be. The Democrats are not as corrupt as the Republicans – Democrats don't lie to themselves about global warming, and sometimes they seem to favor evidence-based reasoning – but it has been a long time since Democrats were the party that truly stood up for blue collar Americans.

In each election cycle, both parties jump through hoops in hopes of fooling voters into believing that the only thing at stake is *values*. On the right, conservative *values*. On the left, liberal *values*. Or libertarian *values*. Or progressive *values*.

"Go to the polls. Vote your brand. Elect your champion. Then go back to sleep."

If I were running as a Democrat, or as a Republican for that matter, I'd have a different message. "America is a country with a cause-and-effect architecture. Always has been, always will be. If we love America, let's do our best to bring out America's best. Let's be partners in Character, partners in Craftsmanship."

And I would campaign for a return to Prosperity Capitalism. I'd campaign for an end to Reagan's Rules. I'd campaign for a revival of FDR's Rules.

And I'd define the election as a referendum on whether the fruits of America's rising productivity belong to the entire workforce, or whether the nation's wealth should be monopolized by those at the top.

That's the broad standard by which I would judge the incorruptibility of a political party. The Republicans flunk my test. The Democrats flunk it too, though not by as wide a margin.

For most of the anti-corruption reforms America needs, the only sure path toward an uncorrupted election process is through the Constitutional Amendment process. Nothing less will be bullet-proof enough to make a difference.

In Article V, our Founding Fathers gave the American people two routes for changing the Constitution. In the standard route, a proposed constitutional amendment is introduced in Congress, and if it passes Congress with a two-thirds vote, it is sent to the legislatures of all the states for their consideration. If approved by at least three quarters of all states, the change becomes part of the Constitution.

The Constitution also provides a second route, one that starts not with Congress but with the states. If two-thirds of our state legislatures issue matching calls for an Amendment Convention, such a convention will be convened and (presumably) all states that wish to participate will send delegates. If delegates to the amendment convention produce a proposed amendment (or two), their proposal(s) will be sent to the legislatures of all the states.

At this point, the second Article V method converges with the first. If three quarters of the nation's legislatures approve the proposed amendment, the amendment is ratified and becomes part of the Constitution.

Given that corruption in Washington is more intense than the corruption in many of our states, anti-corruption activists have argued that the second route has a better chance of success than the first. Winning two-thirds of our state legislature to the anti-corruption cause won't be easy, but it will be easier than winning a two-thirds in the U.S. Congress.

America's habits of political corruption have become so entrenched that our nation now requires two Amendments, a Clean Elections Amendment and a Clean Money Amendment.

Let's start with Clean Elections.

Clean Elections: A Universal Right to Vote

First, it's time to say it straight up, in the U.S. Constitution. "Every adult citizen has the right to vote and the right to be permanently registered to vote. It is the responsibility of the national government and the state governments, together, to protect the voting rights of each citizen by guaranteeing that each citizen will always be registered to vote. The right to vote may be suspended only for those presently serving time in prison."

The Founders weren't ready to embrace a universal right to vote. They were well-to-do white men, and a good many of them didn't want blacks to vote. Nor did it occur to them that women should vote, or even that all white men should necessarily be given the vote. And so it was that the Constitution, given the prejudices of the time, didn't create a universal right to vote.

It's time. A guaranteed right to vote upholds the sacred principle of self-government. Every citizen gets to vote. Agreeing with that principle makes better citizens of us all.

It also eliminates an all too common form of election cheating – scrubbing people off the voting rolls who might vote the "wrong" way. Let's say you're a white Republican election official in a state with large numbers of black and Hispanic citizens. Won't you be tempted to push black and Hispanic voters off the election rolls by using the levers you might have at your disposal? Or suppose you're part of a Republican legislature. Won't your state legislature want to strip all felons of the right to vote, even after they've been released, in order to reduce the overall size of the black vote?

Let's be real. Maybe *you* wouldn't cheat, but it's likely that some of your colleagues will. When abusive practices are implicitly permitted, abusive practices too easily become the norm. It's not healthy to have laws on the books that covertly encourage racial bias in the manipulation of the voting rolls.

This we know. If any state's election laws implicitly allow racial cheating, racial cheating will be practiced. Let's call this evil for what it is. Let's end it, forever, with Constitutional language that requires permanent voter registration for all citizens, with only one exception. Those currently serving time will have their right to vote suspended until they are released from prison.

Clean Elections: Guarantee Equal Treatment for all Voters

Let's imagine America as an honest democracy. Every citizen has the same right to vote as every other citizen. And every election has the same purpose: Identify the candidate with the widest base of public support and award the office to that individual.

But today's America is not an honest democracy. It today's America, the Republican and the Democratic Parties like to pretend that the point of an election is to place members of one party, or the other, in office. That's why so many states use closed primaries. Both parties prefer to cut independent voters out of the loop.

Partisan primaries aren't the Law of God. They are just an option, and maybe not the best option. A significant majority of this country's cities and towns use non-partisan elections to choose their mayors and city councils. In municipal elections, Independents are on the same footing as self-identified Democrats or self-identified Republicans. Non-partisan municipal elections have been around since the early 1900s if not before.

And sometimes they elect capable centrists who would otherwise never have been chosen.

Years ago, John Parr of the National Civic League recounted for me the story of how in 1983 Federico Peña came to be elected Denver's mayor. As Parr told the story, Peña's success was directly tied to Denver's long tradition of holding non-partisan elections.

Denver's Democratic Party was split at the time between two powerful factions. Had the election included a party primary, Peña would have been the odd man out. But with Denver's open primary system, Peña as a centrist was able to pull together a wide coalition and win the election.

As it happened, Peña's election as a centrist greatly benefited the city. At the time of his election, the city had its back against the wall. Its borrowing capacity for municipal bonds was limited, well below three hundred million dollars, while its backlog of capital projects carried a price tag of six hundred million or more.

Mayor Peña reached out to the city's major interest groups. His invitation was simple. Let's sit down with one another, familiarize ourselves with all the city's needs, set priorities, and develop a consensus agenda. Let's jointly agree to a list of projects the city can afford. This is your city; let's all work together to help it succeed.

Thanks in part to the breadth of his base, and to the spirit of respect he encouraged, his working group took its charge seriously, and in time agreed on the ten bond issues the city needed most. Voters approved all ten.[1]

Would a partisan Democrat have done as well? He would have faced longer odds. In Peña's case, at least, the city's non-partisan framework worked to everyone's benefit.

---

1 - Summary drawn from personal conversations with David Chrislip, a facilitator for this process, and from David D. Chrislip and Carl E. Larson, *Collaborative Leadership: How Citizens and Civic Leaders Can Make a Difference*. 1994.

There's a relatively new experiment under way that hopes to apply the virtues of a non-partisan approach to elections that have traditionally pitted Democrats against Republicans. Called the "Top Two Primary," it throws all candidates into the same wide-open primary. The two candidates who perform best in the primary then run against each other in the general election. In red districts, this might pit two Republicans against each other; in blue districts, this might pit two Democrats against each other.

While a promising idea in principle, it can backfire if done too simplistically. Picture a Republican district whose incumbent has retired. Picture a primary race with six or seven GOP hopefuls and only two Democratic hopefuls. In such a scenario, the two Democratic candidates might each tote up more votes than any of the Republicans, and end up facing each other in the general election. A Republican District that holds a Top Two Primary might conceivably elect a Democrat who's not really the district's top choice.

In such a situation, a Top Two Primary would miss the deeper point. The ideal election identifies and elects the candidate with the broadest base of support. Any formula that hands victory to someone other than the most widely acceptable candidate isn't really what we want. A good election has to meet two tests: it has to welcome all comers, and it has to identify and elect the candidate with the widest base of support.

If open primaries are always to meet the second test – identifying the candidate with the widest base of support – they will have to be modified. Rank order voting gives us what we want. If I'm a voter with a ballot in my hand, I will put a "1" next to the name of my preferred candidate, a "2" next to my second choice, and so on.

The polls are closed. The election judges sit down with the ballots and set to work.

In the first round, they award each ballot to the candidate that the voter liked best. Let's say that we're dealing with a primary in which seven candidates have been on the ballot. The goal is to narrow the field to two and put those two in the general election.

The candidate who finishes last is removed from the running. But his or her ballots are still in play – those on which voters also marked their 2nd and 3rd choices and so on.

In other words, those ballots become "second choice" ballots. They are awarded to the candidates who were the voters' second choices.

Again the votes are counted. Again the last place finisher is removed. And again the ballots that have been removed are awarded to the remaining candidates, based on the voter's second choices. (Or third place choices, for ballots that have already been reallocated once.)

The process continues until there are only two candidates left, and those candidates are declared the winners of the primary. We know – because we used rank order voting – that those two candidates enjoyed a broader base of support than anyone else.

It's quite possible that the apparent order of finish will shift in the course of the counting process. Someone with support from a loyal but narrow minority might initially finish first, but be so disliked by everyone else that he's no one's second or third or fourth or even fifth choice. Such a candidate will be overtaken by others who have a much broader base of public support. And isn't that the way it should be? Don't we want our elections to tell us who has the most support and then give us a legitimate method for declaring that person to be the winner?

Those with the most votes at the end of the count are declared winners, and sent into the General Election for their final showdown.

It's a Top Two Primary, yes, but with the safeguard of rank order voting. Nothing is perfect, and this method isn't perfect, either, but it makes more sense than the alternatives. It tells us who's the most popular, and it helps us elect the person whom we know to have the broadest base of support.

Let's experiment with this a bit more, and then find a way to write it into the Constitution. Let's have all primaries be as fair to independents as they are to party members. And let's have all runoffs pit every district's two most popular choices against each other in the general election.

Clean Elections: Honorable Redistricting Rules

The Supreme Court in the 1960s found itself wrestling with the question of whether terrible population disparities among congressional and legislative districts were so questionable that the Court ought to get involved. In Baker v. Carr (1962), a Tennessee case, the Court held that such disparities were justiciable. In Wesberry v. Sanders (1964), a Georgia case, the Court held that population disparities between congressional districts were so great as to violate the U.S. Constitution. In Reynolds v. Sims (1964), an Alabama case, the Court found that population disparities between state legislative districts were in violation of the Constitution. It ruled in Wesberry v. Sanders that congressional districts were to have equal populations; it ruled in Reynolds v. Sims that state legislative districts were to have substantially equal populations.[2]

(As a teen I had seen the issue of population disparities first-hand, if you will. As mentioned in Chapter Three, my dad, Byron Johnson, was elected to Congress in 1958 from Colorado's Second District, which then comprised all of suburban Denver and all of northeastern Colorado, with a total population of 600,000-plus. On Colorado's Western Slope, the state's Fourth District had fewer than 200,000 residents – a three-to-one population disparity.)

Once Wesberry v. Sanders and Reynolds v. Sims had set the national standards, the law of unintended consequences began to take over. The Court's rulings may have created equal

---

2 - All court decisions sourced from Wikipedia.

population standards but they hadn't set any limits on how any state's redistricting process was to unfold.

By tradition, the power to define district boundaries belongs to the legislatures of each state. In a more lethargic era when district boundaries remained much the same from one census to the next, this particular custom hadn't mattered very much. But with the 1970 Census, and every census thereafter, the nation's legislatures were to find themselves in a new era. The principle that voters are to pick the legislators they want got trampled underfoot. Now the nation was in an era that permitted legislators to draw district lines however they chose; in other words, the customary approach to redistricting now gave legislators the power to pick the voters they wanted. The era of modern gerrymandering was under way . . . with a vengeance!

Why has the Congress shown such poor fiscal responsibility from the 1970s forward? Gerrymandering is surely part of the reason. To oversimplify only slightly, highly partisan Republicans reward their constituents with the tax cuts they crave, then use borrowed funds to make up the difference. Highly partisan Democrats do much the same; they reward their constituents by strengthening popular social programs, then use borrowed funds to fill their budget gap. In both parties, incumbents capitalize on the federal government's borrowing power to win re-election.

Reformers in Iowa and California and Arizona have taken this on, with measures that remove responsibility for redrawing district lines from state legislatures and place it with independent commissions instead.

Three states out of fifty, though, or even six or eight isn't very many. Gerrymandering remains a highly contagious disease. It needs to be suppressed everywhere; let's amend the Constitution to make it illegal in all fifty states.

Fast Recap: America's election system is corrupted in three major ways.

Because the right to vote isn't universally guaranteed and protected, election officials imagine themselves to be the Voice of God, entitled to decide personally who shall get to vote and who shall be stricken from the rolls.

Because election rules are rigged in favor of the two major parties, those who would prefer to be independents are systematically discriminated against. Voters who belong to one of the two parties are treated as first-class citizens; voters without a party label are treated as second-class citizens.

Because state legislators now have the power to pick the voters they want, district boundaries are redrawn in ways that systematically discriminate against every state's minority party.

It's time to repair these wrongs. Americans have the right to live under a Constitution that's clean and fair, not under a Constitution that turns a blind eye to areas of systemic corruption.

Let's turn now to the challenge of corrupted campaign financing.

Clean Money 1: Public Financing of Elections

In England, national elections are called by the Prime Minister. Parliamentary districts in England are smaller than congressional districts here, and with a campaign season that lasts only a few weeks, the cost of campaigning is quite modest by American standards. I have heard England's political fund-raising challenge described in the following terms: "At a single wine-and-cheese party, a British candidate can raise enough to fund his or her entire campaign."[3]

---

3 - Paul Miller, then in the Clinton Administration, on a social visit to our home after a trip to the UK.

Such a system has a beneficial side effect. Here, Members of Congress are said to spend four hours a day on the phone raising funds. Members of Parliament get to spend those hours actually studying the issues.

Our election system is so expensive that it forces candidates for office to curry favor from wealthy donors. Result? Almost every law Congress passes will be loaded with favors to major interest groups.

Systemic corruption therefore becomes the norm – an ugly result, to be sure, but locked in. Powerful interests prefer it this way and have little desire to root it out.

If we don't like the result – elected officials in America seriously beholden to wealthy donors – then we as voters will have to get our heads screwed on very differently. For all our dislike of a system that lets wealthy folks get their way, up till now our mood has been much too hoity-toity for us to get behind a fairer way of running things.

Ask almost anyone if they'd be willing to see all campaigns financed with tax dollars and it's likely they will explode. "Let my tax dollars fund campaigns for people I can't stand? Are you *crazy*?"

It's a natural reaction, but not a wise one. With today's privately-funded election system, the entire nation presents its voters with the same unsavory option. Vote for Pre-Corrupted Candidate A? Or vote for Pre-Corrupted Candidate B?

Is that really what we want – candidates in all parts of the nation selling their souls in order to raise the campaign funds they need?

Wouldn't it be a whole lot smarter to have them using public funds to tell their stories and appeal for our votes? So that no matter who we elect, they won't be nearly as compromised by their donor base as they are now?

A political campaign is an extended job interview, right? Imagine that you're a computer programmer and you've been invited to a job interview half a continent away. You'll fly there, stay in a hotel, have your interview, and fly back. Who pays your expenses? Your prospective employer, right?

Isn't that exactly the situation that we, the public, have forced our candidates into? They're the interviewees; we're the interviewers. They want us to hire them to be our elected representatives.

But instead of helping them tell us their stories, as corporate interviewers would, we trap them by insisting that they raise their own damn funds. On the very face of it, aren't we behaving rather badly toward our candidates?

Why is it that America's candidates for public office always have to sell their souls in order to run for public office?

Because we tell them to! What a boneheaded decision.

And what do we reap, for all our boneheadedness? *Precorrupted candidates.* It won't matter who we elect, the votes they cast when we're not looking will always sell us out.

The more corruption we permit within our political system, the more corruption our economy will give us. The more our cities will suffer. The more abuse the natural environment will suffer.

If we are to take the rot out of our system, we will have to begin with its upstream source. We have to begin with the rules that shape the financing of America's political campaigns.

And, before that, we will have to upgrade our own sense of courtesy.

Every candidate that seeks public office is someone's son or daughter. We owe our neighbors the courtesy of listening respectfully to their kids whenever their kids have chosen to run for office, even if they happen to belong to the "wrong" political party. And we owe everyone's sons and daughters the courtesy of publicly funded campaigns.

Most candidates for office, in both parties, would probably prefer to think of themselves as running for public service reasons, without having first to sell their souls. Who really wants to wear a label saying, "Pre-Corrupted Candidate"?

Let's put public financing into the Constitution and throw away the practice of pitting pre-corrupted candidates against one another.

"Pre-corrupted candidates?" Such a terrible idea! What on earth were we thinking?

Clean Money 2: Place Limits on Big Money

In one way or another, large donors will look for ways to buy extra influence. They'll make large donations to political parties. Or they'll run "issue ads" in parallel with a campaign they support. And also when key legislation is up for a vote. And so on. Even with public financing of elections, large donors will still hunger for ways to influence the process and turn officeholders into their private servants.

And one can't trust the Supreme Court to be part of the solution. Too much depends on which party has filled Court vacancies.

At least five kinds of limits have to have to be placed in the Constitution to prevent a corrupted Supreme Court from turning our democracy over to the Top One Percent.

A. Limits on Donations.

It has to be possible to put reins on total donations that individuals make during each election cycle.

B. Limits on Secrecy.

It also has to be possible to put reins on secrecy. The proper rule will look something like this. "No political donation may be committed or spent for any purpose until the donation and its actual donor have become part of the public record, visible to all." Instantly updated donor lists should become mandatory parts of the public record, so that the law can also require "Every political ad shall give its viewers/listeners/readers a direct link to the identities of all its donors."

If corporations or unions spend money promoting a cause, the names of their heads shall appear in the promotion as sponsors and funders of that promotion. The use of dummy front groups shall be illegal.

C. Limits on Influence Peddling.

The third limit has to prevent disguised influence peddling through educational non-profits funded by secret donors. If the Cato Institute or the Heritage Foundation or the Heartland Institute wish to claim that global warming isn't real, that's their right, but their funding sources shouldn't be secret; instant full disclosure should be the norm. No donated funds may be spent for any purpose till the identities of the ultimate donors have been fully disclosed. And the same principle would hold for left-wing think tanks as well.

D. Disclosure Rules for Agents and Bundlers.

The fourth limit has to require full real-time disclosure of agents and bundlers. If Donor A gives twenty thousand dollars to Lawyer Z to be bundled and passed along to Political Action Committee M, all parties to this transaction must be put on the record, and fully identified, before any of the money can be lawfully spent. Should that rule be violated, all donations found to be in violation are to be instantly forfeited to the Federal Election Commission.

E. Disclosure Rules for Foreign Donors.

The fifth limit has to bar the use of foreign funds for

any advocacy that's not done directly in the name of the foreign donor. If Toyota wants to buy an ad that says, "We're Toyota and this is what we think," that's legitimate. If Toyota wants to influence public opinion in America by spending money in secret, using conduits, that has to be illegal.

The more the American public can see the identities of the actual donors, the better. And the Constitution has to make it possible for the Congress to establish limits of this sort.

Clean Money 3: Revolving Door Prohibitions

Yesterday a Senator, today a well-paid lobbyist. Yesterday the Chief of Staff for a Congressman, today a highly paid lobbyist. Yesterday an SEC staffer, today a well-paid employee of a firm the SEC regulates. There's a revolving door, spinning endlessly, that binds together two sets of Washington power players. The capital's permanent lobbying establishment is massive and for the most part quite well-heeled. And the capital's public servants know that good jobs await them within that establishment if they keep themselves within its good graces.

No rational American of any persuasion should feel comfortable with the idea that his or her elected officials – and their staffers – will consistently carry out the wishes of powerful lobbyists in the accurate belief that lucrative lobbying jobs await them the minute they step down from public service.

The Constitution ought to prohibit all elected officials and Capitol Hill or White House staff persons from accepting Washington, D.C. lobbying jobs for at least five years after the end of their service on Capitol Hill or in the Executive Branch.

Fast Recap: America's tools for regulating the role of money in politics fall short on three major counts.

Because our country doesn't support public financing of elections, almost all candidates end up seeking seek funds from wealthy donors. As a result, most candidates are effectively pre-corrupted. Why would we think this is okay?

Large donors have too many back-door ways of influencing the system. There aren't enough disclosure rules and there aren't enough barriers to large donations at key points outside the campaign process.

Revolving door relationships between lobbying firms, office holders, and staffers for Senators and Members of Congress are too easy to create and too tempting to ignore. The Constitution needs to set a high bar and give Congress the tools to raise it even further.

A Clean Elections Amendment. A Clean Money Amendment.

Let's remind ourselves, yet again, of an ancient and sobering reality. With wealth comes temptation, and with temptation the lure of corruption. A wise society chooses leaders determined to keep corruption at bay. A careless society does the reverse.

America's rules have been bent in the wrong direction for much too long. The Supreme Court has bent the rules. Democrats have bent the rules; Republicans have bent the rules. State legislatures across the nation have bent the rules. Wealthy donors have bent the rules. Lobbyists have bent the rules.

The American people will have to fix this, and for us to fix it properly, we will have to write and pass two new Amendments to the U.S. Constitution – a Clean Elections Amendment, and a Clean Money Amendment.

A Clean Elections Amendment needs to guarantee three sets of principles:

- A universal right to vote, in order to halt cheating on the part of election officials.

- Election rules that don't discriminate against Independents, so that all citizens will be on an equal footing.

- Honorable redistricting practices.

A *Clean Money Amendment* needs to guarantee three more sets of principles:

- Public financing, to create unbought candidates.

- Contribution limits, to strip the Top One Percent of its special privileges.

- Revolving door prohibitions, to prevent the indirect bribery of elected officials and their staffs.

America cannot be a democracy of character and craftsmanship until the structural corruptions of our current political system have been outlawed. Nor can it be a democracy of character and craftsmanship until ordinary Americans and wealthy Americans are finally on the same footing.

An Anti-Corruption Proposal for 2020

Here's an action suggestion. See what you think of this as a tool for cleaning up the way America runs elections.

Let's use the presidential primary cycle in 2020 as a vehicle for mounting a nationwide anti-corruption campaign.

I have mentioned that the surer way to develop these two Clean Democracy Amendments is through an Article V Convention. Win approval for an Amendment Convention from thirty-four state legislatures and we can get these two Amendments written, endorsed, and forwarded to the legislatures of all our states for ratification. As with amendments that originate in the Congress, an Amendment originated by an Amendment Convention must win ratification from three-quarters of our state legislatures to become part of the Constitution.

Here's my thought for how this campaign can go national.

Let's begin by seeking to have non-binding referendums added to the presidential primary process in the next election cycle, and every cycle after that till the anti-corruption reformers win the day.

In the 2020 election cycle, my Maryland primary ballot ought to include a question that asks voters if we want the Maryland legislature to endorse an Article V call for an Amendment Convention. The question would be titled, "Anti-Corruption Amendments to the U.S. Constitution." And the wording for the voters would be direct: "Would you like the Maryland state legislature to call for an Article V Amendment Convention, for the specific purpose of drafting one or more anti-corruption Amendments to the U.S. Constitution?"

Voters would be given a brief explanation:

> "America has two ways of initiating a proposed Constitutional amendment – by a two-thirds vote of the Congress, or by an Amendment Convention that's been authorized by two-thirds of our state legislatures.
>
> Any proposed Amendment, whether approved by Congress or by an Amendment Convention, must be put up to all our state legislatures for their ratification. Ratification by thirty-eight legislatures (three-quarter of our legislatures) is sufficient to add a new Amendment to the U.S. Constitution."

A non-binding referendum would be an excellent way for voters to make their anti-corruption wishes known to their state legislators.

The **rules** that shape the financing of America's political campaigns create *pre-corrupted candidates.*

Getting America **UnStuck**
The Politics of **Character** & **Craftsmanship**

Chapter Fifteen

The Hard Work
OF GETTING AMERICA UNSTUCK

"Time to embrace character and craftsmanship."

I OPENED THIS BOOK WITH A QUESTION. "If America were truly a healthy country, what would be different?" And then I examined some of the numbers. The U.S. Congress used to meet high standards of fiscal responsibility but then lost its way. America's senior population is exploding. Social Security isn't ready. America's medical sector is already too expensive to handle the challenge of an aging population affordably and responsibly. Once we had an economy that delivered rising earnings for all Americans, and then the nation's elites flipped a switch. Ever since then, working Americans have been left behind.

America's challenges are growing at a faster pace than our capacity to get thing sorted out. In theory, we look to our political parties to explain the nation's challenges accurately and recommend honorable solutions. In practice, both parties have fallen short.

Yes, America has gotten itself stuck.

An historic turning point has arrived. The quarrels that occupied much of our attention for the last half century don't have a major bearing on the challenges of the decades ahead. Today's social conservatives and today's social liberals know how to go to battle over yesterday's issues, but they're not equipped to respond properly to the challenges of a difficult future.

It's not that yesterday's battles were unimportant. Our social aspirations had gotten out of sync with our social traditions. Were we to be a nation of special privilege for those who were traditionalists – who were white, male, and straight? Or were we to be a nation that would relish its diversity and protect the rights of all?

It wasn't an easy journey for anyone, but in the end the nation found itself settling on a code of equal rights for all, regardless of race or ethnicity or sexual orientation.

It was also an era of rising educational levels for some, and at the same time an era that suffered from the loss of manufacturing jobs. It was, therefor, an era in which those who had gone to college imagined (falsely) that they deserved a brighter place in the sun than those whose traditions were rooted in America's blue collar past. In other words, it was an era in which America mishandled some of its most significant changes; yes, there was a narrative that celebrated an expansion of tolerance, but it turned out to have a dark side. Implicitly it also celebrated an expansion of elitism.

So here we are. The dueling narratives of the last half century, our quarrels over the rights of individuals, have made important differences in our social codes, but at the same time, they haven't been that relevant to America's emerging challenges. Tomorrow's narratives will be put together as a response to new challenges, and they will lead us toward a different vision of how America is to rise to its challenges. The narratives of yesterday had much to do with the stuckness that now ensnares us; the narratives of tomorrow will have to be far-sighted enough to free us from yesterday's snares.

History has given us tomorrow's challenges, even as our politicians continue to champion yesterday's answers.

How are we to reorient ourselves? Let's try this on for size.

We Americans are in the early days of a major shift from narratives rooted in our quarrels over social values – narratives that emphasized both the rights of traditionalists and rights of minorities – to a wholly new set of narratives rooted in the challenges of vast size, vast complexity, and vast responsibility.

We cannot shape a successful response to the challenges of tomorrow from within yesterday's narratives.

Much as it may pain some of us to do so, it would be best to de-emphasize the quarrels over social values and tolerance and individual rights. Most of those have been legally settled, if not yet culturally and emotionally settled. They will continue to shape our sense of who we are, even as they are edged into the background by the larger challenges of tomorrow.

Yes, they were vitally relevant in their day, but the twisting course of History has placed us in new conditions and presented us with new challenges. The narratives by which we take on the challenges of tomorrow will inevitably be different from the narratives by which we wrestled through the key challenges of the last half century.

We live today in an era of vast scale, whose cause-and-effect forces we cannot safely ignore. Everything depends on the business models by which our nation steers its vast capabilities. Choose our business models wisely and we will do well. Choose business models because the forces of systemic corruption have lined up behind them, and it is likely that we will go badly off course.

These tensions have to be recognized and managed responsibly. Some will propose narratives for our future designed to push us off course. Our better narratives will call upon us to rise to our challenges and to our larger responsibilities.

The essence of tomorrow's better narrative can be compressed into a single phrase: "America rises to its full potential when it accepts and fulfills its larger responsibilities."

That's quite a narrative, isn't it? Short, and focused more on the challenges of vast scale than on anything else.

How, one might wonder, are we to fulfill such a narrative? Where does one begin?

The proper answer, as this book suggests, is by embracing a civic ethos of Character and Craftsmanship. Yes, History has placed us in an era of complex systems – systems that rely on cause-and-effect linkages to achieve their aims. When wise business models are used to shape those systems, they will work well, even at vast scale, and Americans everywhere will enjoy their benefits.

On the other hand, when careless or even corrupted business models are used to shape the vast systems of our time, it is likely that those business models will cause damage, probably at great scale, and leave us with a weakened nation.

By what narrative shall we respond to these challenges?

What would our wisest moms recommend?

They'd recommend an expanded narrative of responsibility, wouldn't they? Wisely-designed systems generate beneficial consequences. Folks no longer fling ashes against anyone's white sheets. In America's emerging narrative, we listen to the voice of conscience; we accept responsibility for the wisdom of all the major systems that weave our nation together.

There's a knack to creating wise and beneficial systems, just as there's a knack to driving a football team all the way to a touchdown. Our narrative calls us to accept our larger responsibility, and then it invites us to develop the knack of fulfilling those responsibilities as well as we possibly can.

Neither of today's major parties is qualified to weave together the sort of narrative our nation requires. Both parties are habituated to narratives that rationalize short-sighted ways of seeing the world.

Narratives that have been formed for the purpose of rationalizing special privilege will not help any of us rise to the challenge of meeting our larger responsibilities. We need a larger narrative that advances the national interest, not a dueling set of partisan narratives that care not a whit for the national interest.

In other words, a narrative of Responsibility will work best when honorable Americans from all points of view are invited to contribute to the shaping of our nation's future.

The partisan habits of yesterday's quarrels may have been relevant to our clash over cultural values. They won't be that useful in the face of History's new responsibilities.

Complex systems cannot be improved without wise input from Americans of all viewpoints. The proper management of an era of vast scale requires a civic ethos of collaboration and mutual respect. That's the general rule.

But yes, there's a stumbling block ahead. America is not just a land of complex systems and their far-reaching consequences. America is also a land of systemic corruption that has taken hold in high places.

Our guiding narrative needs to acknowledge the challenge. Yes, temptation is eternal. Yes, corruption is a choice. Yes, we serve the nation by shutting down the forces of corruption. And yes, if we are to bring systemic corruption to a halt, we shall have to teach ourselves to discuss it openly and honestly.

There are those on the Left who will argue that America's corruption is rooted in its loyalty to capitalism. I disagree. Capitalism can be a source of honest dynamism for America if we are willing to outlaw its corrupting inclinations. Just because we don't want baseball stars using steroids doesn't mean that we plan to outlaw baseball. Just because we don't want capitalist businesses engaging in systemic corruption doesn't mean we want to outlaw capitalism altogether.

Conversely, there are those on the Right who will argue that capitalism works best when left alone. There's not a shred of evidence from the past four or five centuries that actually supports this claim; the lessons of History are quite clear. Capitalism always works better when it's forced to operate from within responsible rules.

There's an artistry to creating wise rules that bring out the best in any capitalist economy while at the same time suppressing its darker inclinations. And that's History's challenge; that's where tomorrow's guiding narrative needs to take us. Shut down the systemic corruptions of capitalism's darker practitioners; bring out the best in our capitalist way of life; steer our capitalist economy toward an ethos of serving the national interest; steer American capitalism toward the restoration of Prosperity Capitalism. "America best realizes its larger potential by first rising to its larger responsibilities."

This has not been our track record in recent years. We have looked the other way as systemic corruption has taken hold and ripped up the protections that used to help American workers share in the nation's rising prosperity.

In giving us a narrative of Responsibility for vast scale and wise business models, history also pushes us into a battle for America's soul. Will America be a nation that lets itself be run over by the forces of systemic corruption? Or will America be a nation that fights them off, that restores its capacity for outlawing irresponsible conduct?

Our first hurdle is the "polite company" problem. There is a code among America's elites that no one is allowed to speak of systemic corruption in polite company. It's just rude. It's not unlike the idea that no one in the slave South was allowed to state the obvious – that the slave economy was deeply immoral and dreadfully dehumanizing. And it's not unlike the practice within Boston's Catholic hierarchy – before the Spotlight team pulled back the curtain – of hiding the reality of pedophilia. One doesn't admit to systemic corruption when it has become an integral part of the dominant culture.

But we Americans cannot anchor ourselves in a civic ethos of Character and Craftsmanship without at the same time making it clear that the practice of systemic corruption has to end. It has no role in America's better future.

In our era, the "Polite Company" problem also pervades our universities. The economics departments of our land will never admit that they teach their students to run interference for the forces of systemic corruption. And, of course, the "polite company" problem also pervades the mainstream media. Who besides Amy Goodman has the freedom to call out the deeply internalized censorship of America's official culture?

But just because so many of our media figures have been conditioned never to use the words "systemic corruption" doesn't mean that it doesn't exist. The reality is that the forces of systemic corruption are doing quite well, thank you, and they don't want to be overthrown. They know that the power they wield is illegitimate. They know that they're in it for themselves; they're not in it to advance the national interest. They know that their corrupted banking system crashed the economy, and they're not especially sorry. They know the world can't afford to stay with fossil fuels, but they're not that interested in being part of the solution. They know that America's medical sector has been gouging the American people for half a century and they love the results. They know that the nation's leading Republicans and many of its leading Democrats eat out of their hands. Why would they want to change a thing, even though nothing in their agenda advances the larger well-being of our nation as a whole?

We have to pick this fight if we are going to win the change that America needs. We have to make the topic of systemic corruption an issue that everyone acknowledges, and we have to put its defenders on the defensive. We have to help the American people see the problem for what it is, so that all Americans can participate in its solution.

It does us no good to equate capitalism with systemic corruption. What we want is a capitalist economy in America that has been liberated from systemic corruption, a capitalist economy that serves the national interest. We want a culture of Character and Craftsmanship among our entrepreneurs, within our workforce, within our unions, and within our political parties. "America fulfills its larger promise best when it accepts and insists on fulfilling its larger responsibilities"- that's the narrative that takes our entire nation forward.

Hollywood made it easier for all of us to raise this issue, when it gave us three films in 2015 that focused on questions of systemic corruption with surprising clarity. *Spotlight* told the story of how the systemic corruption of the Boston Archdiocese was exposed by a team of investigative journalists at the *Boston Globe*. Of the fifteen hundred priests employed by the Boston Archdiocese, almost ninety turned out to be pedophiles. Had the Archdiocese faced up to this problem and dealt with it responsibly? No. The Archdiocese had kept it covered up. It had turned systemic corruption into a way of life.

The *Globe* had already run a number of stories on individual priests who were guilty of pedophilia, but it was the story that cast the problem as one of systemic corruption that finally forced the Archdiocese to come clean.

Concussion tells a similar story, by focusing on the medical examiner who began to suspect that the NFL was covering up a widespread problem of serious brain damage among its former players. Here, too, was a story of systemic corruption, with a powerful industry doing its best to keep the truth from coming out.

In a different way, *The Big Short* also tells a story of systemic corruption. It shows us the final months of the housing market, whose collapse triggered the failure of Bear Stearns and Lehman Brothers and others. An entire industry had chosen a corrupted path and no one in charge ever blew the whistle. A few far-sighted individuals realized, well in advance of the crash, that they could get rich by selling short large pools of mortgage-backed securities. And they did. You just wish, at the end, that industry regulators had been half as foresighted as the short-sellers featured in *The Big Short*.

Systemic corruption in the Boston Archdiocese. But no one knew how to name it for what it was, and so for years no one really saw it. Systemic corruption in the NFL, hiding the story of severe brain damage, chronic traumatic encephalopathy, for as long as it possibly could. Systemic corruption in the housing market, systemic corruption in the mortgage-backed securities market, systemic corruption in the ratings industry – but no one could speak its name, no one could turn it into a challenge to be solved, and so, in the end, the markets collapsed and millions were thrown out of work. Why? Because it was against the rules for anyone to talk openly about systemic corruption and its hold on an entire industry. That which we dare not name is something against which we will find ourselves defenseless. How many thousands of children were sexually abused by their priests, in the Boston Archdiocese and its sister archdioceses around the globe? Silence in the face of systemic corruption is a terrible mistake. It always has been. It always will be. And yet we live in a culture of enforced silence.

The historical forces that have made America a nation of vast scale have also made America a nation that tolerates systemic corruption. Now we are challenged by the forces of History to shift our guiding narrative. No longer can we be a people who maintain their silence in the face of systemic corruption. We need to become a people with a civic ethos that helps us find our way to a wiser and better future.

The larger narrative of our era can take us toward a much brighter future, if we accept its challenge. *America fulfills its larger promise by accepting its larger responsibilities.* It's a narrative that none of us should walk away from. It's the narrative by which America realizes its greater promise. Get our systems wrong and we'll get America's future wrong. Get our systems right and we get America's future right.

It's a narrative that ought to speak just as strongly to America's conservatives as to America's liberals. The cause-and-effect world in which we live affects everyone equally. Leave it in squalor and we all suffer. Clean it up properly and we all prosper.

The story of the Spotlight team is a story of ethical and intellectual heroism. And that's the story that our emerging narrative invites us to emulate. Let's become a public of Character and Craftsmanship; let's become a public of ethical and intellectual heroism. *An America that accepts its larger responsibilities will become an America that fulfills its higher promise.*

The path of Character and Craftsmanship is the path by which we – the American people - can help America achieve its full promise. It is possible that many of us will resist this path, at least at first. But in the long run, we will come to realize that History's emerging narrative deserves our full attention. It is the only path by which America realizes its full promise. We will be quietly proud of ourselves for having chosen it.

"America fulfills its larger promise by accepting its larger responsibilities."

History has given us a new narrative. Let's be grateful, and let's make it work.

Fudge Factor Americanism is what *keeps* us stuck.

Character and **Craftsmanship** will *get* us unstuck

★

Acknowledgments

SOMETIMES IT CAN TAKE A LIFETIME to bring a messy situation into proper focus. America has long been a nation that lurches forward in fits and starts; it offers so many ways to pursue partial reform, but for the most part we fall short of recognizing the larger wisdom that America also needs from its people. That sense of larger wisdom eluded my undergraduate education; it wasn't present in the various causes I embraced over the past half century; it certainly hasn't been nourished by the partisanship of recent decades. Let's face it: the public intellectuals of today have fallen short.

One who knows about the founding of our republic remembers with some awe the talents of Alexander Hamilton, James Madison, Benjamin Franklin, and George Washington. The pressures of nation-building called forth extraordinary thinking from our nation's Founders, just as the pressures of leading a nation out of slavery called forth Abe Lincoln's extraordinary leadership skills. Such examples are vital but rare. Once again America has reached a turning point in its history, but for the present, the political leaders we have simply aren't the political leaders we need.

It has always been a bit too easy for the naturally ambitious to muscle their way to the front, regardless of how ill-suited they may be for History's deeper demands. Why was it that the American South suffered so long from a weak economy and low personal incomes? It should be obvious. Those who were the region's leaders couldn't imagine themselves investing properly in the education of all the region's young people, and especially not those who were black. So the South remained backward for decades because its leaders couldn't stand the idea of turning their region into an engine of equality and advanced learning.

And why is it that America is responding so poorly, even today, to the challenge of global warming? Again, our dominant tradition is one of small-minded leadership. "Let's do things the way we have always done them, even if we're wrong."

Why haven't we a stronger tradition of stepping up to our nation's most difficult challenges? Why is it that we so seldom ask ourselves the larger questions about America's core challenges and what it will take to bring out our country's greater promise? Somehow too many of our thought leaders like to pretend that America's most important questions were answered in its Founding, and our only mission now is to live within that same framework today.

And that has become our contemporary curse. Though we have built a nation of great promise, we haven't developed a political system that teaches us to take the long view.

I have written this book in hopes of showing us how to lift that curse, and it is time to express my appreciation to so many who in different ways have helped me in this effort. "If we knew what we were doing, what would be different?" There's no marked path for someone anxious to answer that question. Fortunately, in my unmarked journey I have received lots of wonderful help along the way, and it is time to acknowledge at least a few of those who enriched my efforts in so many ways.

Without knowing it, even from an early age I had signed on for what Malcolm Gladwell has called the "Ten Thousand Hour" rule. Those who are destined to become truly good at something will find themselves working at it, obsessively, until their skills truly mature – a ripening process that requires of its devotees at least ten thousand hours. Gladwell cites various examples, from Microsoft's Bill Gates and Sun's Bill Joy to the

Beatles, those whose "overnight" successes were preceded by years of obsessive toil, often starting in their early teens if not before.

I fit Gladwell's general profile, I suppose, though in my case ten thousand hours wouldn't have been nearly enough.

My acknowledgements will have to be the acknowledgements of a lifetime. I wasn't testing a known idea, so I couldn't have been tutored in any normal way, and there's no fraternity of intellectual guides that I might salute. Instead what I will do here is acknowledge many decades of enrichment. So many have helped me sharpen my sense of how the world works, and to imagine better visions of how it might work. Here I will name only a sampling of an extended group from whom I have learned and by whom I have been inspired.

No one asked me to write this book; I have written it from an inner need. Painters have to paint, sculptors have to create statues, singers have to sing, dancers have to dance. And philosophers have to philosophize? Yes, that too.

Allow me to introduce a lifetime of friends and associates, those from whom I have drawn inspiration and with whom I have matched wits.

1940s and 1950s.

My parents were my first and surely my most important influence. Kay Teter and Byron Johnson first met in the Baptist youth group at the University of Wisconsin, and through the influence of its two pastors, L.B. Moseley and Shorty Collins, became lifelong member of a national Christian pacifist organization, the Fellowship of Reconciliation (FOR). As kids, we'd find ourselves being hauled along to FOR conferences again and again. Those were settings that brought together quite an extraordinary band of activists and leaders. One of their FOR friends, the Reverend Glenn Smiley, was to serve as Dr. King's right-hand man in the Montgomery bus boycott. After the boycott ended, successfully, Smiley took to the road to spread the word. He visited our family in Denver, and over a three-hour supper, debriefed my parents on the ins and outs of the Montgomery boycott. I was thirteen at the time, I think, a wide-eyed kid who grasped only a fraction of the discussion unfolding in our dining room.

In 1947, my dad had earned his Ph.D. and received a teaching offer from the University of Denver. So there we were, living in cramped quarters in the middle of the postwar GI housing boom on the nation's campuses – my dad, my mom, my infant sister, and me. Crowded housing was everyone's issue, in those days. Soon my parents and some of their faculty colleagues had decided to form a coop housing association. They'd put up their own savings, borrow money, buy property, and build themselves the kind of community they really wanted. After three years of work, it all came to pass. Our housing coop of 32 homes opened its doors in 1951. South Dahlia Lane was a wonderful neighborhood then, and it still is. Our architect, Eugene Sternberg, had incorporated many of Frank Lloyd Wright's design ideas, I would eventually learn. But I was only seven when we moved in. What did I know?

It wasn't long till it became obvious that my dad had politics in his blood. In 1952, he jumped in and ran for the state legislature. Over his career, he would run for public office ten times, losing five and winning five. He served one term in the Colorado state legislature (1955-56), one term in Congress (1959-60), two terms on the University of Colorado Board of Regents (1971-82), and one term on the board of Denver's Regional Transportation District (1983-84). He ran as a liberal Democrat, but once in office he always saw himself as a servant of all the people, regardless of party.

In addition to the hats he wore as a professor and as a politician, Byron was also an active lay churchman, serving on any number of committees and commissions for the United Church of Christ, and when called to do so, preaching lay sermons. For him, civic involvement was all of a piece. He served his neighborhood, his church, the state of Colorado, and the nation. He served in secular roles; he served in religious roles. Advancing the civic good was his calling, and by turns he did so as a churchman, as a professor, and as an elected official. (And, as a good Swede, he had jokes to share no matter what sort of setting he might find himself in.)

My mom, Kay Johnson, served in her own way too, working for many years in the office of the American Friends Service Committee in Denver, supporting its antiwar work and its nuclear freeze campaign. In their passion for relevance, Byron and Kay put a stamp on me that has lasted my whole life. "Whenever we find ourselves living in a world that hasn't been put together properly, lean in. Criticize the status quo. Push for a better way of doing things."

I didn't always agree with their choices, but I always admired their commitment and their desire to bend the arc of history toward America's higher promise.

That sort of commitment was modeled for me by their friends as well, especially their FOR friends, and I also owe thanks to such leaders as John Swomley, Glenn Smiley, Bayard Rustin, Martin Luther King Jr., and so many others who were part of their FOR family.

Neighborhood was important too. South Dahlia Lane, our housing community, was a wonderful place to grow up in the 1950s. Two of my buddies from those days are still among my most important friends, Paul Danish and Hugh Calkins.

1960s.

The larger conversation about our country's journey and its destiny intensified when I was an undergraduate at Harvard. I learned so much from so many, and want to give special mention to Stan Katz, my excellent history tutor, and to Tom Staley and Gibbs Kinderman and Todd Gitlin and Robb Burlage and Chris Hobson and Gail Falk and so many others.

Those were the years when quite a few students from Harvard and Radcliffe left their studies to travel south and lend a hand in the nation's struggle for civil rights. John Perdew, also from Denver, was arrested in Americus, Georgia, along with three others, who were then charged by the state of Georgia with sedition, a capital crime. In other words, they were at risk of being convicted and executed. In time, the charges were set aside and they were released, but all who became civil rights activists were always in danger.

Given my upbringing and the temper of the era, I was inevitably drawn to the SDS, Students for a Democratic Society, which in its earliest years pursued a relatively quiet set of activities. Its most prominent goal was that of awakening a poor people's movement in northern cities, in hopes of developing a nationwide poor people's movement. From those years I remember with special fondness the leadership of Al Haber, Barbara Haber, Tom Hayden, Lee Webb, Jim Monsonis, and a great many others.

In time, as the US intensified its air war in Indochina, slaughtering innocent peasants at the rate of hundreds or even thousands per week, the fury of the student antiwar movement became so ill-tempered that I pulled back. By an odd set of coincidences I found myself in the University Christian Movement from 1966 to 1969. Acknowledgements are due to Henry Bucher and Charlotte Bunch and Leon Howell and Paul Schrading and Nell Sale and Mal Davis and many others.

1970s.

In 1969 I landed back in Denver, newly married to my first wife, Nell Sale, and seriously clueless about the type of graduate work that might one day become my calling. I signed up to drive a taxi for Denver Yellow Cab, and soon found myself a member of its newly-accredited drivers union, the Independent Drivers Association (IDA). I was to stay at Yellow Cab till 1980, rising to become president of the drivers' union and in 1978 winning approval from its members for a driver buyout of the cab company.

There were so many in the IDA who contributed in different ways. Kudos go to Ben Stone and Ron Von Dollen, to Bill Hosey and Tom Hanlon, to Ed Cassidy, Walt Smith, Jerry Ziegler, Connie Wood and Jerri Dulin and Keith Mangrum and LaVerne Roberts and many others. Special mention goes to our attorney, Ike Kaiser, for all his help and council along the way.

My years in Denver involved me in other community projects as well. My gratitude goes to John Duggan and Nell Sale and Bernie Jones and Skye Moody and many others.

1980s.

Eventually I realized it was time for me to get an MBA and set aside any idea that I was meant to imitate my dad and pursue a Ph.D. in economics. I landed at Stanford's business school for two remarkable years, and remember with fondness so many wonderful people, from Jerry Norman and Kelly Teevan and Clare Swanger to Jonathan MacQuitty and Jerry Porras and Jan Orloff and many others.

The early 80s were a time of many turning points, most notably the stroke of good fortune by which Martha and I met. We were married in 1983, and the chance to be part of her extended family made our union even more special. Just as it was her good fortune to become a Johnson, it was my good fortune to become a Nace. My gratitude extends to her parents, Ted and Lovina, to her siblings Julia and Ted and Kelley, and their extended families of aunts and uncles and cousins galore.

In early 1983, Martha and I bought a house together, in Jamestown, New York, and went to work for Cummins Engine Company at its Jamestown Engine plant. It was a special company in so many ways; let me give special shout-outs to Greg Swan and Bob Reed, acknowledging at the same time all the talented and hard-working people who make Cummins such a remarkable company.

From Cummins I went to Bain for three years of consulting work. I have fond memories of Mark Gottfredson and Anne Glover and many others.

1990s.

There are many ways to do consulting, and after Bain I spent four stimulating years as a consultant in the telecom industry under Gemini Consulting's broad umbrella. My gratitude for those years goes to Tom Gage and Dave Trapani and Jack Prouty and a number of others.

We relocated several times during these years, first to Jamestown, then to Boston, and then to Annapolis, Maryland. Our two children were born in the late 1980s and the adventures of parenting were upon us. Martha signed on with the Clinton Administration in 1993, and it fell to me to explore the pleasures and the challenges of being a PTA dad. There were many colleagues in these adventures, including LynnDee Conley and Mary Alice Gehrdes and Terra Snider and Tom Frank and so many more.

These were the years when Milt Jaques, from our church, introduced me into a long-running faith-based discussion group to which he belonged, held together by the able leadership of Tony Downs. Tony has been the discussion group's *convener extraordinaire*, and regularly prevails upon the Brookings Institute to set aside private dining rooms for these gatherings. Whenever I attend, I marvel at the exceptional insights that these discussions always generate.

2000s.

In the early 2000s, I found myself working for Education Resource Strategies, building complex spreadsheets for school systems in Los Angeles, Boston, and elsewhere. As mentioned in my chapter on schools, my appreciation for these enriching years goes to Karen Hawley Miles and Stephen Frank.

Also in the early 2000s, several of us who had been friends

at Bethesda-Chevy Chase High School back in the fifties found ourselves reconnecting. There was much to lament about George W. Bush's ill-advised adventures in Iraq and we used email the way elders of previous generations had once used rocking chairs and shaded porches. But I also got to share some of my writing efforts with these dear friend. Special thanks go to Friedner Wittman, Ed Levine, Elizabeth Kessel, Howard Bond, Dick Brown, J. D. Eveland, Leslie Fox Kefauver, Sally Dublin Slenczka, and others in our post-high school circle.

In 2006 I was invited to join the Parole Rotary Club of Annapolis. I nodded, and before I knew it, I was a Rotarian. What a wonderful group of men and women, not just in the Parole Rotary Club, but in Rotary Clubs all over the world! Our club's fund-raising efforts generated cash support for any number of local service non-profits. Meanwhile, our signature project, Books for International Goodwill (BIG), kept clicking along, collecting book donations locally, not only from individuals but also from local school system. The best of all those donated books are shipped overseas to bolster the libraries of school systems and communities. The books themselves are free but the recipients are expected to pay shipping costs. Think of it this way: a twenty foot container is filled with twenty thousand books and sent to a school somewhere in Africa or Asia. The school pays BIG $4,000 for shipping costs, which translates into a net cost of only twenty or twenty-five cents a book. Over the years, BIG has sent out several million books in this way – it's quite an exceptional service!

There are so many fine Rotarians that I will limit myself to mentioning just three of the very best. Steve Frantzich is the club's globe-trotting book merchant, hitching his role as book peddler onto his far-flung travels as a political science professor for the U.S. Naval Academy. Joyce Edelson has been the spark plug that keeps BIG's book warehouse from slipping behind. And Bill Fine has been the Parole Rotary club's spiritual leader, helping one and all to keep their sights on Rotary's far horizons.

The challenge of finalizing my own book led me to withdraw from Rotary not all that long ago, but I continue to treasure Rotary for the fellowship and the service it promotes.

2010s.

No expression of appreciation would be complete without a nod of thanks to those who have hosted our neighborhood coffee shops. Carla Lucente led off as our neighborhood's first barrista, and she has been ably followed in that role by Mark Abrahamson. Their wait staffs have been exceptional; all who have sipped coffee first at Carla's Bistro and now at Mark's Bean Rush know just how special they have been.

Martha and I have been privileged to be a part of First Presbyterian Church of Annapolis, and of the extraordinary community that our church has brought together. No one played a larger role in pulling things together back in the nineties than Dick Cobb, who spearheaded a decade-long demolition and renovation project, fondly remembered by everyone as the church's "Sweat Equity" era, but our church has also been well-served by our first-rate pastors, Bill Hathaway and Heather Shortlidge, by our extraordinary choir director/organist Bob Muckenfuss, and so many other capable staff members and volunteers.

And it has also become an increasing privilege to live in our corner of West Annapolis. So many fine neighbors – from Terry and Betsy, to John and Ann, to Linda and Jerry, and more than we can count.

The Larger Wrapup

My deepest gratitude goes to my family, to my sister Christi and my brother Eric, for their love and support, to my wife Martha and to my children Anna and Lucas, who have never allowed me to become so wrapped in my work that I forget everything else. They kept me grounded in life's best moments, their various passions turning me into a ballet dad and a viola dad and a baseball dad and a rock band dad and a youth orchestra dad and so much more.

America will come out of the 2016 elections in a very bad mood, I fear. And who will step forward with the insight our nation requires? Our pundits? No. Our Republicans? No. Our Democrats? No. Across the board we will see troubled Americans reworking the nation's issues by adding even more fuel to this nation's emotional flames. We hardly realize how badly out-of-date our political habits have become.

I have spent a lifetime observing all sorts of battles. In some cases I have seen truly wonderful people ask themselves, "What's Missing?" and then put together truly exceptional answers. In too many other cases, though, I have seen America's politicians and its business leaders and its pundits find ways to keep our nation wrapped around the axle.

As a people, we are not unlike the six blind men who famously tried to describe an elephant. "It's a wall." "It's a rope." "It's a spear." And so on on.

Every perspective has had a measure of validity; very few of them truly move us forward.

So. What's missing? With us, as the American people? What is it that hasn't found its way into our repertoire of responses?

We have had a hard time coming to grips with the realities of our cause-and-effect world, and with the responsibilities it creates.

If ours were a civic ethos of Character, a civic ethos of Craftsmanship, I believe we'd do better at accepting our responsibilities.

And that's the difference.

A people that shirks its responsibilities will inevitably experience America as a nation of dark and difficult challenges.

A people that steps up to its responsibilities won't have as gloomy an experience. Yesterday's dark challenges – once reshaped – will become tomorrow's bright opportunities.

But first there is a switch we have to flip. We have to become a people of character and craftsmanship.

This isn't just my insight. It's the distilled insight of my parents, and my larger family, and so many friends over the years. We live in a world of cause-and-effect systems; if we allow ourselves to heal them when they malfunction, yesterday's darker challenges become tomorrow's brighter opportunities.

It's an insight that opens into a larger prayer. "Dear Lord, please quiet my heart. Please help me sense my calling. Please help me to become part of Your Solution."

My life has been blessed with flashes of heart and wisdom of so many different kinds. My thanks to all who have shared so much. Knock on wood. The adventures ahead will help all of us bring out America's best.

CPSIA information can be obtained
at www.ICGtesting.com
Printed in the USA
LVOW05s1437020317
525946LV00007B/50/P